The Phoenix Guitar Company

Guide to
GUITARMAKING
FOR THE SMALL SHOP
A Step-by-Step Approach

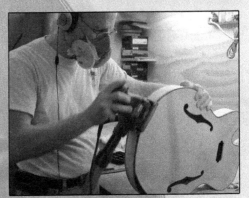

George S. Leach

The Phoenix Guitar Company's Guide to Guitarmaking for the Small Shop: A Step-by-Step Approach

Published by Wheatmark®
1760 East River Road, Suite 145,
Tucson, Arizona 85718 USA
www.wheatmark.com

ISBN: 978-1-62787-252-2 (paperback)
ISBN: 978-1-62787-253-9 (ebook)
LCCN: 2015930943

This book is dedicated to my guitarmaking students.
I hope they will enjoy it, use it to go on and make more guitars,
and maybe enjoy it as much as I do.

CONTENTS

PREFACE

This book was written for several reasons. First, it came from a basic need to document our process. While taking a class on small-shop production from Charles Fox several years ago, Charles mentioned the need to have procedures be well documented. A luthier should not count on his memory because he will often forget something and have to waste either time or materials when steps are taken out of order. I've certainly made this mistake many times, each time swearing that I'd document our steps (or sometimes just swearing) but not getting around to it.

Second, in our guitarmaking classes, we have needed a good description of our processes so our students would have something to follow and take home to study. We referred them to several excellent books, but we felt that it would be best to properly document our process and have a book that describes exactly how we do things here at the Phoenix Guitar Company.

Third, we make three very different types of guitar: steel string, archtop, and nylon string (both crossover and classical) guitars. With a small shop, we were forced to find commonality between these types of guitars and minimize the unique steps so we could build all three styles of guitar and not be buried in different procedures and jigs. We thought a book describing a process for the different types of guitars could be useful.

ACKNOWLEDGMENTS

Many people are responsible for helping with this book. First, my wife, Connie, who has been so supportive and encouraging all along, even back when I cracked the kitchen counter doing my first fret job. Next, my former business partner, Diana Huber, without whose collaboration this would not have been possible. Also, all the great luthiers from whom I have had the opportunity to take classes: Dick Boak, Bill Cumpiano, Tom Ribbecke, Frank Finnochio, Dale Unger, Grit Laskin, and Charles Fox. They have all been so willing to share their ideas.

In addition, I want to thank the many other fine luthiers who have been great in sharing of their knowledge through either conversation or permission to use their ideas from their websites: Mike Baranik, Michael Bashkin, Bob Benedetto, John Greven, Kevin Ryan, and Kathy Wingert. I also want to thank Monica Cable for her help in editing my manuscript. Lastly, I want to thank my daughter, Jennifer McMahon, who painstakingly put together all the drawings in this book. We spent hours huddled over rough sketches or my incomprehensible descriptions, and thanks to her knowledge of CAD, she turned them all into great drawings.

I want to give a special thanks to my good friend Dennis Ramsey, for spending so many hours helping me set up my new shop (for about the 6th time) in Torrance, California. Finally, my family, some of whom are mentioned above: My wife, Connie, my son Rob, my daughter Jennifer, my son-in-law Mark McMahon, and our two beautiful granddaughters, Hayden and Addison. They all have made my life very special.

INTRODUCTION

There are many ways to build guitars and many different books out there describe the process. We will describe a practical way to make three different types of guitar (steel string, archtop, and classical) using similar methods and jigs for all of them. For example, we believe that the main differences between a steel string and a classical guitar are very simple. The bracing, wood thicknesses, and some dimensions are different, but the basic construction can be mostly the same. Even though many classical guitars are built using the Spanish method, which is totally different from most steel string construction methods, many classical builders build some of the finest guitars in the world using a dovetail neck/body joint that can be effectively used in steel string guitar construction.

Now, there's no way to avoid making the top and back plates on an archtop guitar. Whether you decide to carve them or steam and press them, those steps are simply different from any steps for steel string or classical guitars. However, once you get past that part of the construction (along with the top braces), many of the rest of the steps are the same (or very close). Binding, neck carving and fitting, fretting, finishing, setup, and so forth are very similar, and with few exceptions you can use the same procedures and jigs in the process.

People have often asked us why our neck joints are dovetails. Although we have used bolted-on necks for both nylon and steel string guitars in the past, we found two things that changed our process. First, our classical customers didn't like the idea of a bolt-on neck. We didn't think it made any significant difference in sound, but they simply didn't like it. So we changed our classical and nylon string crossover guitars to dovetails. Second, our archtop guitars were already dovetails because we didn't see a good way to bolt on an archtop neck (there may be one, but none of the options sounded good to us). This meant that two out of the three types of guitars we made had dovetails and one had bolt-ons. We didn't like mixing our processes like this, so we decided to make the steel string guitars with the same neck joint as our other two types of guitars.

So, this book will describe steel string, classical, and archtop construction, showing as much similarity between the construction of each as possible.

EQUIPMENT

Through the course of reading this book, you'll see all the equipment we use. There are many ways to build a guitar, and it may not be necessary to obtain all the equipment that we use. However, a few things are critical in any shop and should be taken seriously.

- Dust control. Don't skimp on this. You should always have a good system and use it whenever you're using a band saw, table saw, router, or any piece of equipment that will create dust (which is just about all of them).

- A good dust mask. No matter how good your dust control system is, some dust gets into the air. A good dust mask is cheap and provides excellent protection.

- Hearing protection is also very important. The kind many gun shooters wear works well in a shop environment.

- A good fan for your spray booth and good ventilation. I've walked into many shops and just about fainted from the fumes. At least try to protect the customers who come into your shop.

- Thickness sander: I think this is important. Thicknessing all your woods by hand is very prone to error, and is also very time consuming. A tool like this can help make the job of thicknessing tops, backs, sides, bindings, etc. very accurate, fast, and not dependent on you having a "good day". You don't necessarily need an expensive one (though they're all somewhat costly), but they will turn a time consuming, error prone job into a snap.

- Bandsaw: You don't need a huge bandsaw. A 14" bandsaw can handle virtually all your needs (as it does mine). It can resaw up to 12" (9 " is all I've really needed to resaw), and it doesn't have to break the bank.

- Sanding machines: Both a belt sander and a disc sander are important. Many belt sanders have a combination of both in one. You'll see what we use in the book, and I don't know a luthier without at least one.

- Router table: We use a router table a lot, from truss rod slots to shaping necks and bridges. Get the best one you can afford.

- Table saw: In guitarmaking, we mainly use our table saw for cutting fret slots, bridges, and end grafts. However, we often use it for making jigs, benches, etc. However, many luthiers use them more than we do. You need to decide for yourself if this is a need for your shop.

- Other equipment: We'll let the book speak for itself here. You'll see what we use, and can decide how you should set up your shop for yourself.

I'm sure there are more, but also realize that you don't necessarily have to create everything from scratch. It's easy to buy a preslotted radiused fingerboard and save the expense and time of doing it yourself. Steel string and classical bridges can be purchased, as can archtop bridges and tailpieces. There's nothing wrong with becoming familiar with the basics of getting a guitar built before you dive into all the little details.

HOW TO READ THIS BOOK

I try not to repeat myself (too much) in this book. For example, I try to give a thorough description of the construction of a steel string guitar. For the archtop, I don't rehash the binding process. I use the same equipment, and the steps are all the same. I don't go back over the carving of the neck because it's described in detail once. If you're carving a neck with a different profile, create a profile template and start carving—it's pretty much the same process. I try to go into detail on those parts of the guitars that are truly different: creating classical braces, carving the archtop plates and archtop braces, and making a fingerboard extension for a raised fingerboard for both the archtop and classical, in this case. I only cover the finishing process once and only cover grain filling once. So, if you only want to build a classical guitar or an archtop guitar, you'll have to read most of the sections on the steel string because the construction, as far as this book is concerned, is very similar.

PART ONE: THE STEEL STRING GUITAR

DRAWING 1.1.1 The Steel String Guitar

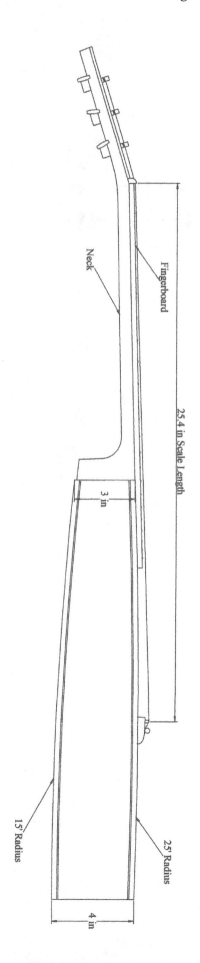

DRAWING 1.1.2 The Steel String Guitar Braces

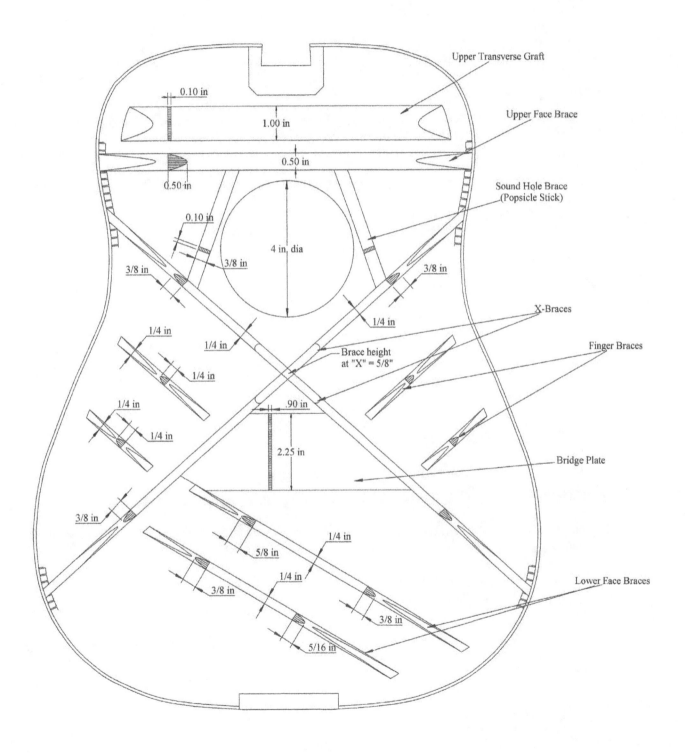

1.1
THE STEEL STRING TOP

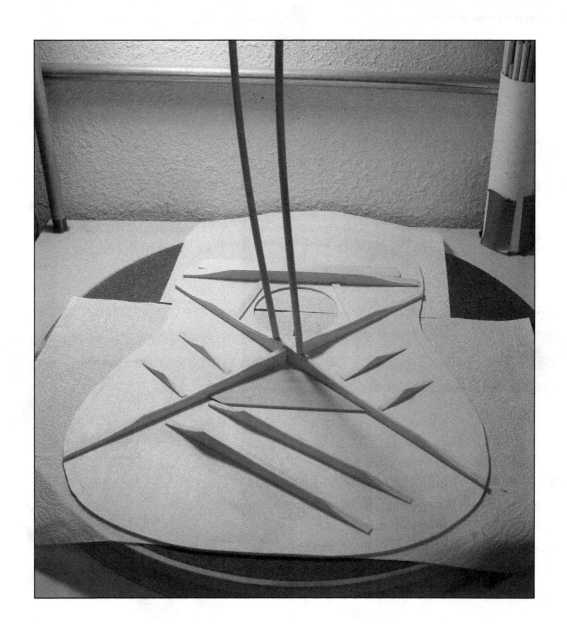

TOP PREPARATION AND GLUING

The steel string guitar we are making for this book is a thin-body dreadnought (one inch shallower than a standard dreadnought)—mainly for playing comfort. Our customer ordered it with African mahogany sides and back and an Engelmann spruce top. We will describe our method for preparing a steel string top.

FIG. 1.1.1 We start with a beautiful book-matched set of Engelmann spruce and sand its thickness down to about .150".

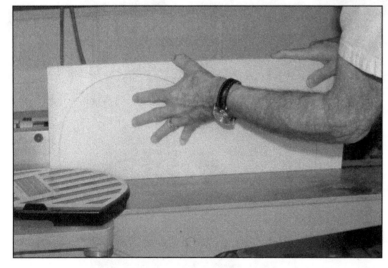

FIGURE 1.1.2 Next, we put both halves together. Make sure the edges that are to be glued are down against the jointer table. Then we joint the edges.

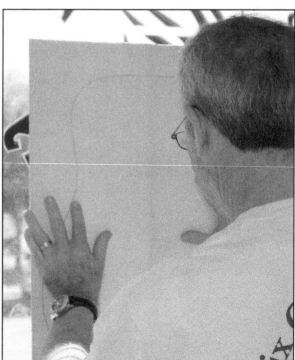

FIGURE 1.1.3 After the edges are jointed, they are "candled" or held up together to a window to check the edges for fit. Sometimes the edges have to be rejointed, but after candling, no light should shine between the halves of the top.

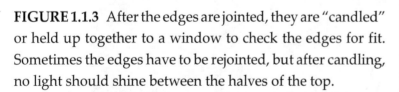

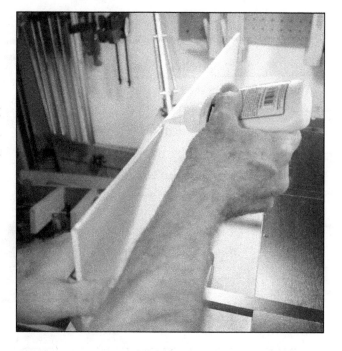

FIGURE 1.1.4. Once we are happy with the candling results, we put glue (in our case, we are using the red label Titebond Original Wood Glue) on one edge as shown.

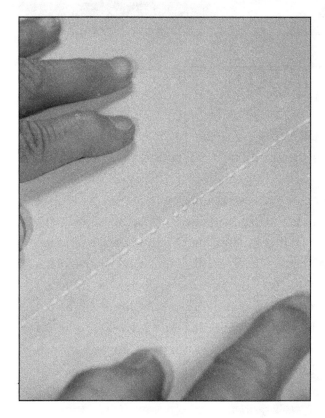

FIGURE 1.1.5. Now we put the top halves together on the top of the plate-gluing jig (we got ours from LMI, although they're also easy enough to make yourself). Always check for good glue squeeze-out along your joints.

FIGURE 1.1.6. We place a strip of wax paper under the glue joint and then put the frame over the halves of the top, tying the ropes around the ends of the frame ends.

FIGURE 1.1.7. Finally, we put wedges between the ropes and the frame. This will do two things. It will pull the two sides together and push the halves of the top down, making sure neither side climbs up during the gluing process. After you put the wedges in, tap them with a rubber mallet to be sure they are seated as well as possible.

THE STEEL STRING ROSETTE

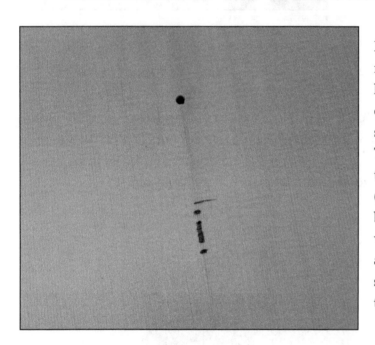

FIGURE 1.1.8. Once the top is glued, we'll determine the position of the sound hole. The small hole (3/16″ in diameter) in the figure marks the center of the sound hole, and the next mark (a slash) denotes the outside edge of the sound hole. The next three marks are two thinner black marks that show where 1/16″ wide black/white/black (b/w/b) strips of purfling will be. Sandwiched between them is a wider mark where a 3/8″ cut will be made. This will allow for a 1/4″ strip of abalone shell (abalam in our case) framed on each side by a 1/16″ strip of b/w/b purfling. Note that there is a 1/8″ spacing between the marks.

FIGURE 1.1.9. The inside radius of the abalone ring is 2 3/8″, so we set a compass for that radius.

FIGURE 1.1.10. After drawing both the inside radius of 2 3/8″ and the outside radius of 2 5/8″ onto a piece of abalam (it's difficult to see the pencil lines in the photo), we will cut out multiple pieces to form the abalam arc. We will cut well outside the lines to allow for any error.

FIGURE 1.1.11. Here are a couple of typical pieces of the arc. We prefer to work with multiple short pieces rather than a few long ones. They are easier to get the final radius sanded onto and are easier to inlay.

FIGURE 1.1.12. In this photo, we are sanding the inside radius of one of the abalam pieces.

FIGURE 1.1.13. This is the jig we made to sand the outside radius. Note that this jig is very similar to the one described by Bill Cumpiano in his book Guitarmaking Tradition and Technology. The lower piece of particleboard is the base. The middle piece has the inside radius (2 3/8") cut into it to hold the abalam piece after its inside radius has been sanded. The top piece has a small piece of rubber band glued to its edge. It will be turned over and used to clamp down the abalam piece during sanding. The rubber band will help us hold the abalam piece in place.

FIGURE 1.1.14. Here is the jig in use. The top two pieces of particleboard are clamped together with the screw on the top, and they pivot with the 3/16" pin. Once the jig is set up, it is very easy to make multiple pieces with the same outside radius.

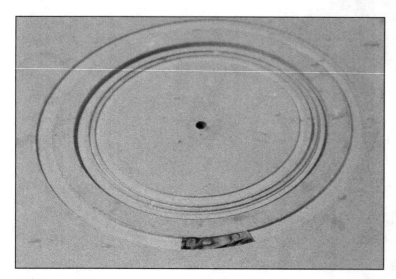

FIGURE 1.1.15. The first piece has been put into a jig that has a 1/4" slot routed in a circle with the proper radius. We will use this jig to hold all the pieces of the final arc and see how they fit together.

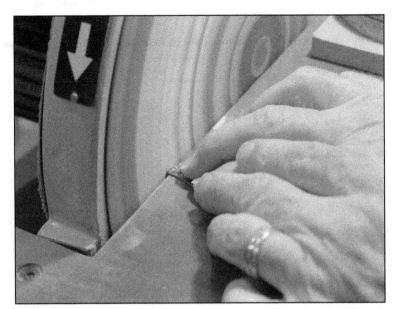

FIGURE 1.1.16. We sand the edges as needed so they align perfectly.

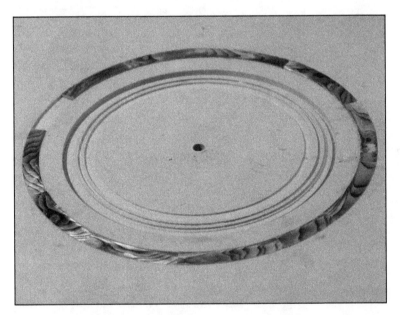

FIGURE 1.1.17. Here is the final abalam arc. Edges are all sanded to match and are ready for inlay. The arc is not going to be completed into a full circle because the open section will be hidden under the fingerboard. It would be a waste of good material to glue it under the fingerboard where it would never be seen.

FIGURE 1.1.18. We will now cut the grooves into the top using a laminate trimmer attached to a Stew-Mac circle cutter. The laminate trimmer base had to be slightly modified so the holes in the circle cutter screw properly into its base.

FIGURE 1.1.19. A 3/16″ pin is put through the center hole, and extended down into the backing board shown in figure 1.1.18. A 1/16″ bit is in the router and is set to cut to about 2/3 the height of the purfling. Now we set the bit at the point marked as the inner purfling ring and cut.

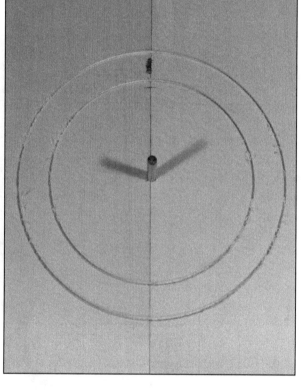

FIGURE 1.1.20. The inner and outer purfling rings have been routed. Now we have to change the bit in the router to a 3/8″ bit and set the depth to that of the abalam thickness.

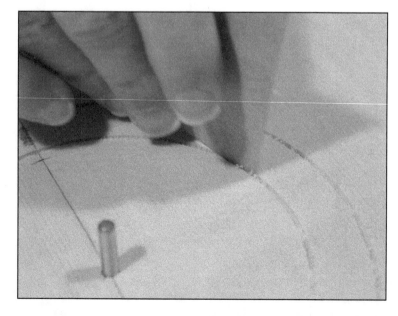

FIGURE 1.1.21. Before routing the next groove, we sand the first two grooves with 220-grit sandpaper. We'll sand the top and down in the groove to completely clean up after the cut. We don't want one of the wood fibers to get caught on the laminate trimmer as we make the next cut. If it is caught, it could cause a tear-out.

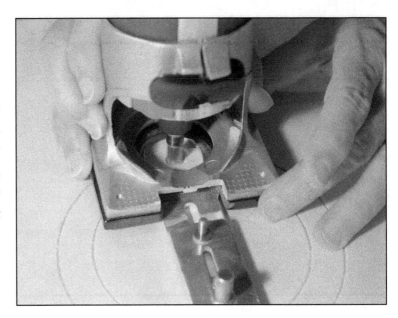

FIGURE 1.1.22. The section of the arc that will be directly under the fingerboard can be used to test the placement of the center circle. If it's slightly off, it can be adjusted and reset and retested. When it's right, we cut the inner circle. After cutting, we sand it to clean up our work.

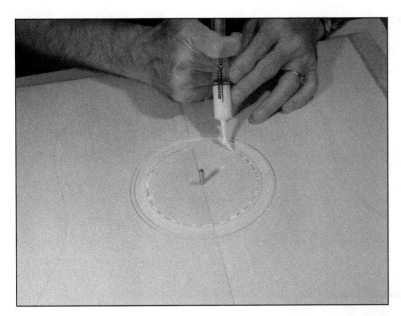

FIGURE 1.1.23. Now, we put some Titebond into the inner groove. We are using a plastic syringe. Note the slot does not have to be completely filled with glue. This would make the slot swell and lead to the purfling piece not properly fitting. A little glue will do just fine.

FIGURE 1.1.24. The b/w/b purfling is being put into the slot.

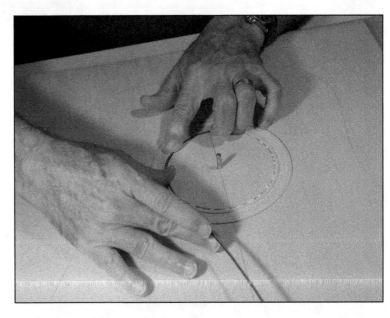

FIGURE 1.1.25. After putting the purfling strip into the groove, snip it off with a nipper. Note: if this entire first ring will show and not be partially hidden under the fingerboard, you must make a good miter joint. If the joint will be hidden under the fingerboard (as in our case), don't spend extra time mitering the joint. Just nip the purfling and move on.

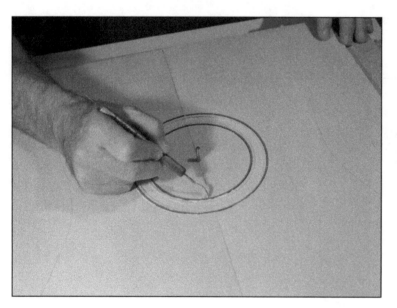

FIGURE 1.1.26. After putting in the outer purfling ring, clean up the glue before inlaying the center ring.

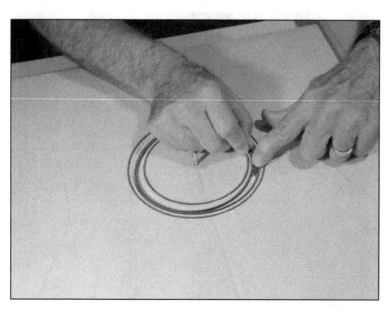

FIGURE 1.1.27. To inlay the inner ring, put the outer and inner pieces of purfling in place and get the first piece of abalam in place. Don't worry about glue yet. Then, glue next to the first abalam piece (only enough to glue one piece), put the second abalam piece on top of the first, and slide it along the groove in place. This process is followed until all the pieces are in place. At this point, the initial piece can be slid out of place, glue put underneath, and slid back.

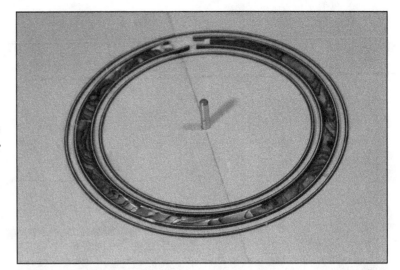

FIGURE 1.1.28. Here is the final rosette. Now, clean up the glue and let it all dry for a while.

FIGURE 1.1.29. After the glue dries, we sand the rosette and get the top sanded to its final thickness (about 0.105 to 0.110″). Then we put the 1/16″ bit back into the router and cut the sound hole (leaving about 1/8″ inside the inner edge of the inner purfling ring).

Note: we only slightly sand the top surface to level the rosette. Additional thinning will be done from the back side of the top.

PREPARING AND GLUING THE TOP BRACES

FIGURE 1.1.30. Now, we focus on the top braces. We start with a piece of very nicely quartersawn Engelmann spruce that matches the top wood.

FIGURE 1.1.31. Next, we will saw off a few pieces of the brace stock—each a little over 1/4″ (actually, a little over 5/16″ to be safe). After sanding, we want the braces to be 1/4″ wide.

FIGURE 1.1.32. Using a template, we transfer the bracing pattern to the underside of the top. Note that we have drawn the lines very lightly in pencil so they can be easily erased or sanded out later.

FIGURE 1.1.33. Once the braces have been thickness sanded down to 1/4″ (which is the desired width of our braces), we begin preparing the X braces by first drawing a 25′ radius onto one edge of the braces. The top of this guitar will have a sphere with a 25′ radius, which, from our experience, helps in tone and structural integrity.

FIGURE 1.1.34. Now, we sand the drawn radius onto the bottom of the braces.

FIGURE 1.1.35. We have a template of the top of each of the braces. It is time to draw the top pattern onto each of the braces and cut it roughly on the band saw, leaving plenty of room for error.

FIGURE 1.1.36. Using the belt sander, we get the final brace down to the pencil line. Note: this is still slightly oversize. We will get to the final size after the braces are glued down.

FIGURE 1.1.37. The shape of the guitar must be cut out on the band saw before we glue braces down. This should be a very rough cut, staying about 3/8″ outside the actual line of the guitar tracing.

FIGURE 1.1.38. The X braces will be prepared first. We put them over the tracing on the top and mark the bottom brace where they intersect.

FIGURE 1.1.39. The final height at the intersection of the X brace will be 5/8″. We will mark the brace at the 5/8″ point, and we will also mark it at about 15/32″. This is the point where we notch the brace to keep the bottom brace about three-quarters of the total height and therefore as strong as possible at the X.

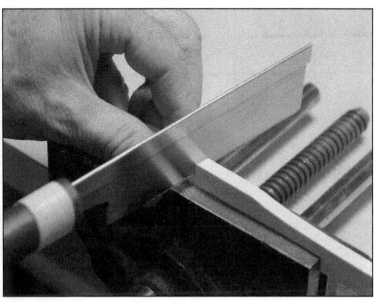

FIGURE 1.1.40. After clamping the brace into a vise, we use a fine kerf saw to cut the brace down to the 15/32″ line at the angle traced onto the brace.

FIGURE 1.1.41. After cutting both lines, we use a chisel to cut out the center part.

FIGURE 1.1.42. We set the upper brace into the lower brace slot and mark the sides of the top brace in preparation for notching.

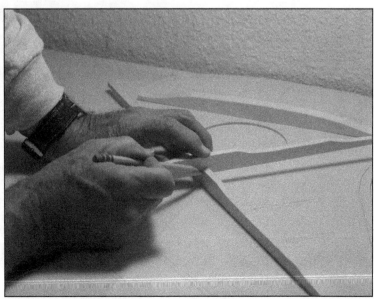

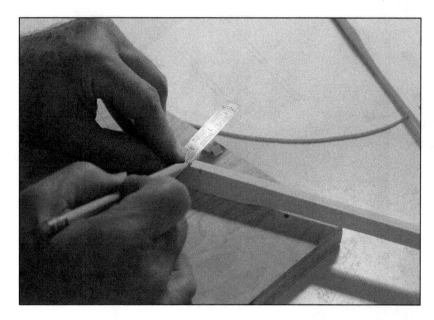

FIGURE 1.1.43. Now, we bring the marks on the side of the top brace across the bottom of the brace.

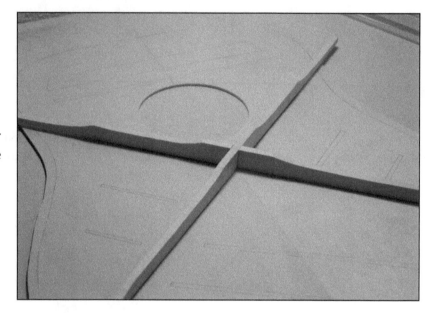

FIGURE 1.1.44. After cutting and chiseling the top brace, the final X looks like this. It's ready to glue.

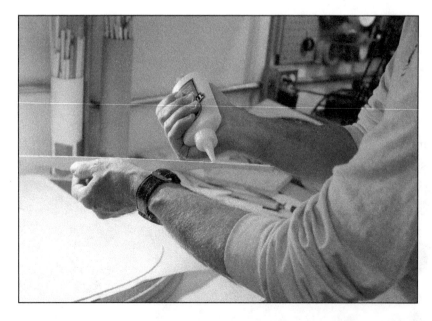

FIGURE 1.1.45. Applying glue to the bottom brace.

FIGURE 1.1.46. Both braces glued and ready for go-bars.

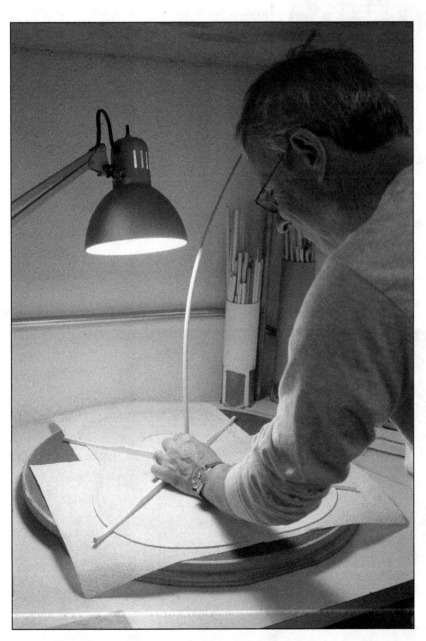

FIGURE 1.1.47. The first go-bar goes in the center of the X.

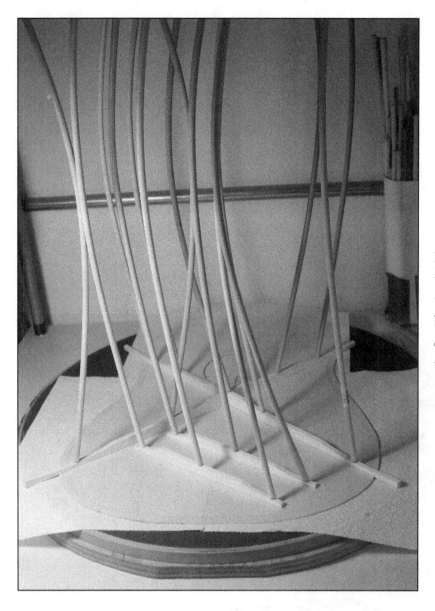

FIGURE 1.1.48. We complete gluing the X and glue the lower face braces, which were made the same as the X braces. Now we use our glue scraper to clean glue squeeze-out and wait before we glue down more braces.

FIGURE 1.1.49. We use the leftover scrap from the guitar top to cut out the upper transverse graft. Note the direction of the grain is lengthwise to the brace. This is important. This brace will be glued with its grain perpendicular to the grain of the top. The main purpose of this brace is to keep the top from splitting at the edges of the fingerboard as it dries out.

FIGURE 1.1.50. Here are the finger braces. They are 1/4″ tall and have been preshaped on the sander. Note that the grain is vertical, as it is on every brace on both the top and back of the guitar (except the bridge plate— its grain orientation is not important),

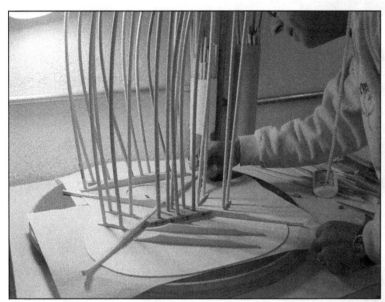

FIGURE 1.1.51. Here is the top with nearly all remaining braces (including the bridge plate) glued down. We clean the glue squeeze-out.

FIGURE 1.1.52. Finally, the sound hole braces are being made. These small braces strengthen the area under the rosette. They are made from scrap left over from the top. We glue one on each side of the sound hole, forming a pentagon shape with the X braces and the upper face brace.

CARVING THE TOP BRACES

FIGURE 1.1.53. Finally, it is time to carve the braces. We have made the job much easier by pre-shaping much of the brace material before gluing the braces down. First, we carve the intersection of the X brace using a small flat-soled plane. As mentioned before, this brace will be 5/8″ tall at this point.

FIGURE 1.1.54. Now we carve the legs of the X braces using a curved-sole plane. A chisel can also be used, but our experience shows that we are more accurate using the plane. The brace will be 5/8″ tall at the center and remain flat for about 1.5″ or so, slope down to 3/8″, and remain at that height until about 3″ from the edge of the top. At that point, we slope it down and keep it at 1/8″ until the guitar edge. Note that this is how we carve our braces. We do not scallop our braces as many builders do. We have had excellent tonal results from this method (having compared our sound with many other guitars) and have not had any issues with bellying.

FIGURE 1.1.55. The braces must now be thinned by planing the upper corners. This takes away very little of the brace strength, but it does take away weight, which would otherwise just make the top work harder to move with the vibration of the strings. Making the braces thinner helps increase overtones that help in the overall tone of the instrument. After planing, we sand the tooling marks and make the brace smooth.

FIGURE 1.1.56. We use a chisel to thin the edges of the finger braces. Again, this is not removing much strength but is removing a lot of the mass of the brace.

FIGURE 1.1.57. Finally, we will use the curved-sole plane to slightly scallop the straight edges of the finger braces—again, this is just removing unnecessary mass.

FIGURE 1.1.58. Here is the top, nearly done. We are gluing a small spruce piece over the gap on the bottom X brace—just for added strength. After it is glued and dried, it will be planed and sanded to blend in with the contour of the braces.

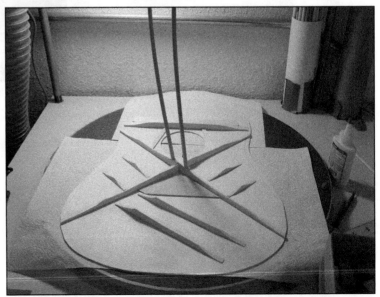

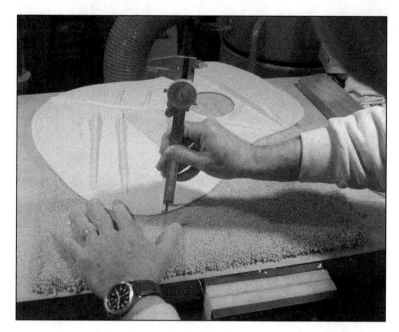

FIGURE 1.1.59. One very important point is to make sure the outer wings of the X braces, as well as those of the upper face brace, are planed down to no higher than 1/8″. This will be important as we get the top fitted to the sides and kerf.

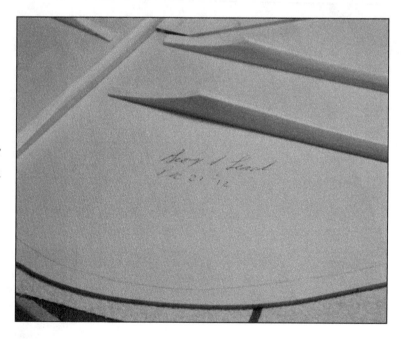

FIGURE 1.1.60. Finally, sign and date your work. Don't use any kind of pen that could stain through the guitar top (like a felt-tip marker).

1.2
THE STEEL STRING BACK

In this chapter, we go through the preparation of the guitar back, from resawing to thicknessing, gluing, and brace preparation.

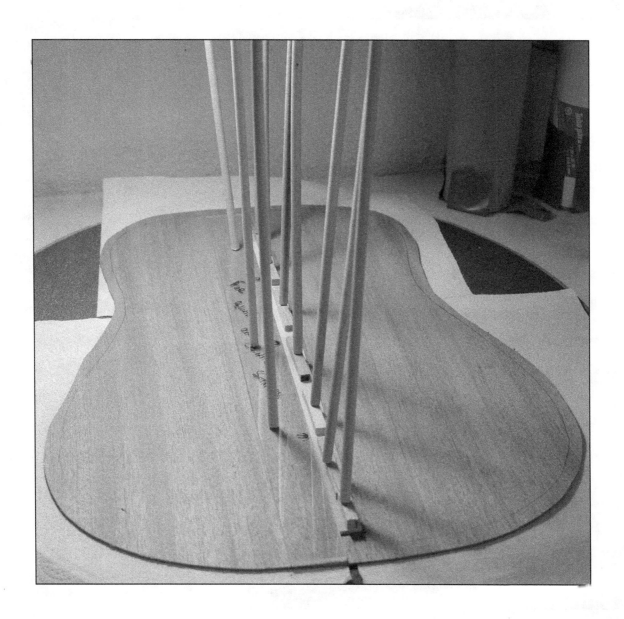

═══ PREPARING AND GLUING THE BACK ═══

FIGURE 1.2.1. The customer for this guitar wanted African mahogany for the sides and back. In this photo, we are resawing the back from a quartersawn board.

FIGURE 1.2.2. We sand the pieces for the back to about 0.150″ in thickness before gluing.

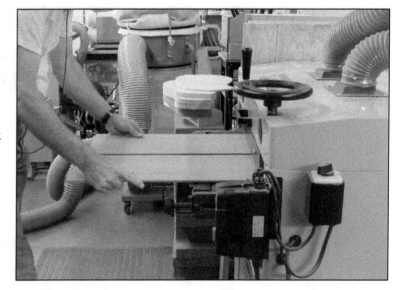

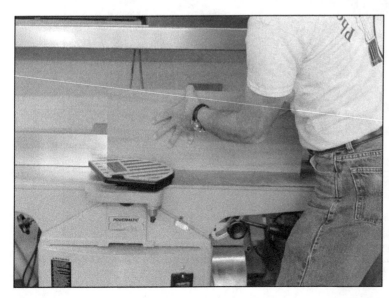

FIGURE 1.2.3. As with the top, the edges of the back that will be glued together are jointed. Both pieces of the back will be jointed together.

FIGURE 1.2.4. After jointing, the edges are held together and are candled, just as we did with the top.

FIGURE 1.2.5. Now we apply glue to the back edges.

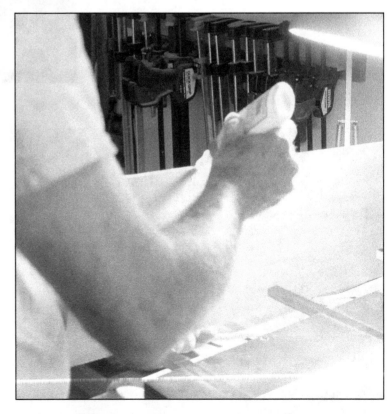

FIGURE 1.2.6. We use the plate-joining jig to glue the back together.

FIGURE 1.2.7. After we put the back halves together and put the bracket over them, we use ropes to tie the bracket down.

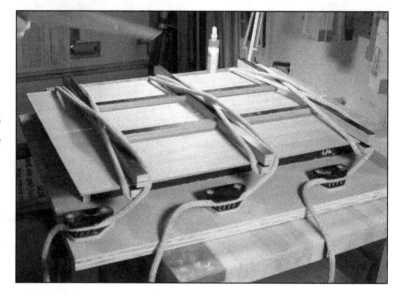

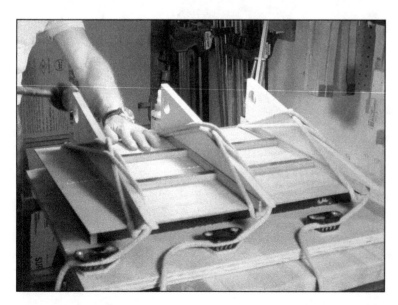

FIGURE 1.2.8. Wedges are slid between the ropes and the bracket and are lightly hammered in place with a rubber mallet. Now we wait until the glue is dry.

══ PREPARING AND GLUING THE BRACES ══

FIGURE 1.2.9. After it is glued, the back is thickness sanded to between .100″ and .105″ (Note that this is our preference. Some luthiers use different dimensions.) This should give us a final dimension of about .090″ to .095″. We roughly cut the shape on a band saw—about 3/8″ oversized. Next, we use a piece of scrap from the guitar top to make the back strip, which is being shown here in the go-bar deck. Note that the grain of the back strip *must* be perpendicular to that of the back. Its strength should be in holding the back joint together, and if the grain is in the same direction as the back grain, its purpose would be defeated. We use a back strip that is 5/8″ wide and long enough to reach from the headblock to the endblock. In the photo, you can see that we go-bar down a piece of plexiglass and then glue down the center strip against it. The plexiglass holds the center strip in the correct position. In addition, we draw a centerline directly down the glue line of the back to ensure that the center strip is exactly on the centerline.

FIGURE 1.2.10. After the center strip is glued, the back is clamped to a bench and double-thick masking tape is put down each side of the strip.

FIGURE 1.2.11. We use a very small hand plane to plane down the edges of the center strip. This step will tear out many facets in the strip that will be sanded out in the next step.

FIGURE 1.2.12. We use 120-grit sandpaper to smooth out the strip and shape it from a rectangle to an arc.

FIGURE 1.2.13. This photo shows the center strip, sanded and ready for back braces.

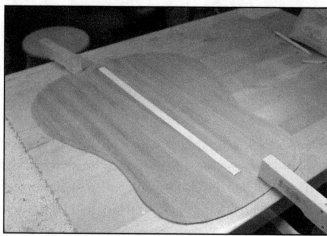

FIGURE 1.2.14. Here are the back braces in their correct placement (again, different luthiers place them differently). We put one directly at the waist and one at the upper bout. The other two evenly split the distance between the waist and the endblock. The braces are shaped in the same manner as those on the guitar top—except these have a 15' radius on the bottom.

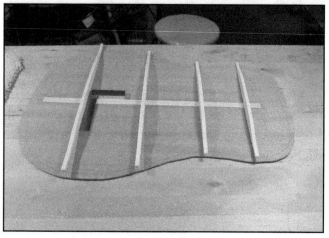

FIGURE 1.2.15. We need to be sure the braces are perpendicular to the center strip, so we will use a right angle to position each brace.

FIGURE 1.2.16. With the brace held firmly at 90 degrees to the center strip, we will use a sharp pencil to mark each side of the brace on the center strip.

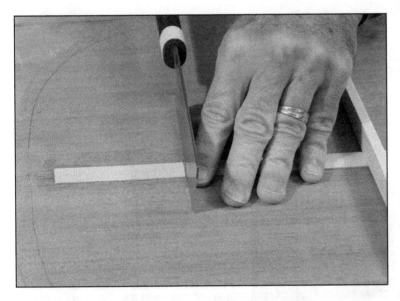

FIGURE 1.2.17. Using a thin kerf saw, we cut just inside the lines. If you cut exactly on or outside the lines, you will have gaps between the braces and the center strip.

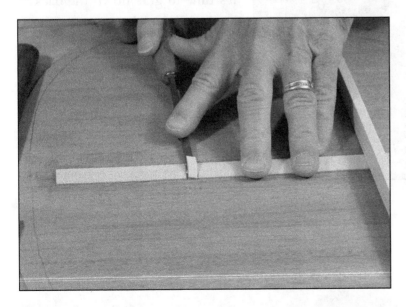

FIGURE 1.2.18. After cutting inside both brace lines, use a thin chisel to remove the center strip wood, being careful not to tear out any of the back wood in the process.

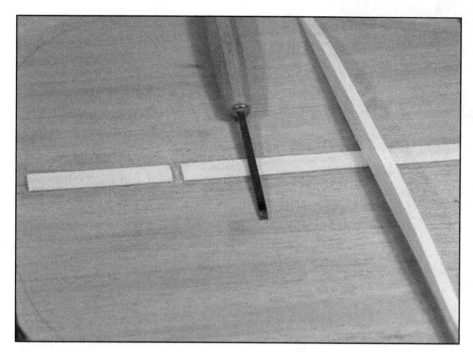

FIGURE 1.2.19. Use the chisel to remove all the wood and excess glue from the slot. When we glue the brace in, it must sit evenly on the wood of the back.

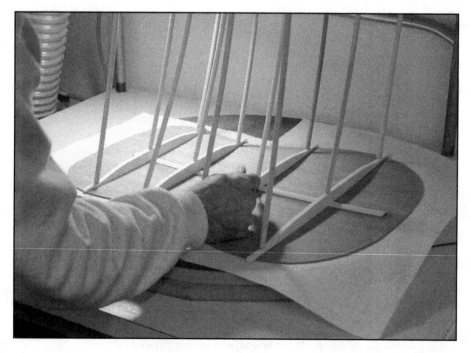

FIGURE 1.2.20. Once all four slots are cut and cleaned out, it's time to glue down the back braces. Remember to use the 15' hollow form under the back during this step.

CARVING THE BACK BRACES

FIGURE 1.2.21. Using a small block plane, each brace is carved down using a plane to a height of 5/8" in the center.

FIGURE 1.2.22. All the brace ends are carved down to 1/8", where they will tie into the kerf.

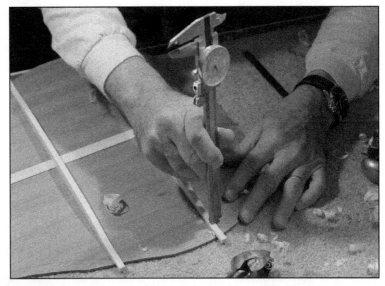

FIGURE 1.2.23. Finally, a plane is used to shave material off the sides of the braces, and after a little sanding, the back is ready.

1.3
THE STEEL STRING GUITAR BODY

In this chapter, we will discuss all the remaining steps in making the guitar body, including bending the sides, gluing on the top and back, bending and profiling the sides, and gluing on the bindings.

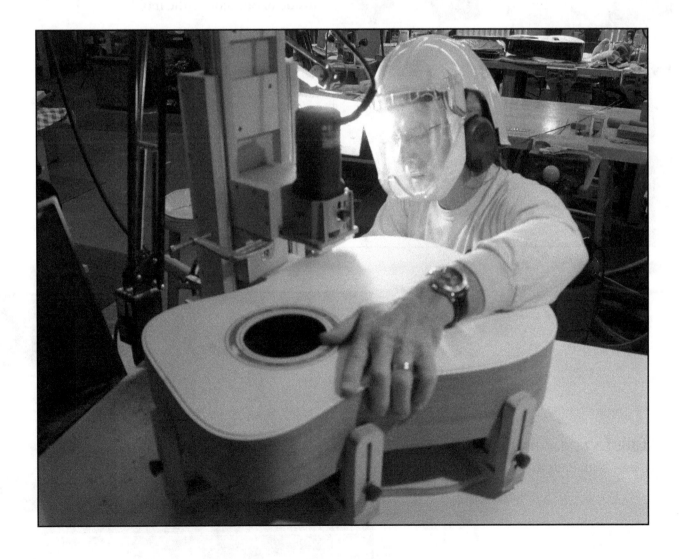

$$=\equiv\equiv\equiv\ \text{BENDING THE SIDES}\ \equiv=$$

FIGURE 1.3.1. We are using a dreadnought mold and will put a piece of masking tape along the inside of one side of the mold.

FIGURE 1.3.2. Mark the important spots on the tape—both ends and the waist.

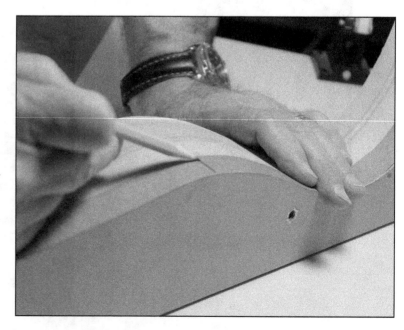

FIGURE 1.3.3. Put the tape on one side that is already cut a little longer than the tape and thickness sanded (or "thicknessed") to 0.085". Then we transfer the lines from the tape to the side.

FIGURE 1.3.4. The outside face and the guitar top are marked with pencil. This is repeated on the other side. It is a bad mistake to discover that you didn't pay proper attention to the book-match of the sides and realize you have bent one side wrong. You'd then have to straighten the side out and rebend it.

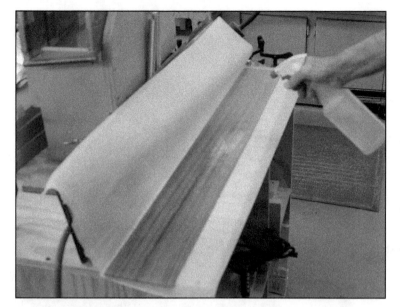

FIGURE 1.3.5. The side is folded into a sheet of parchment paper and sprayed with water on both sides. It does not have to be soaked. You can't see it in the photo, but we marked the parchment paper showing the exact location of the guitar waist.

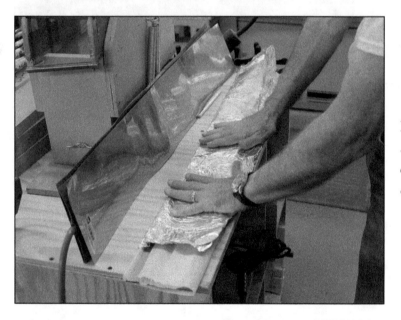

FIGURE 1.3.6. We now fold aluminum foil around the parchment paper. Again, the exact position of the waist is marked clearly on the foil.

FIGURE 1.3.7. We create a sandwich with the foil between the two pieces of spring steel, using a heat blanket directly against the foil. Again, we mark the position of the waist.

FIGURE 1.3.8. The sandwich consisting of the sides, paper, foil, steel, and heat blanket are inserted into a Fox bender. This bender was developed by Charles Fox and has become an industry standard, especially among small builders.

FIGURE 1.3.9. The main waist clamp is lowered until it is snug with the side sandwich. Next, the springs are connected to the waist crossbar. This crossbar is critical, especially for narrow-waisted guitars with figured woods. It helps prevent the wood from splitting at the waist bend.

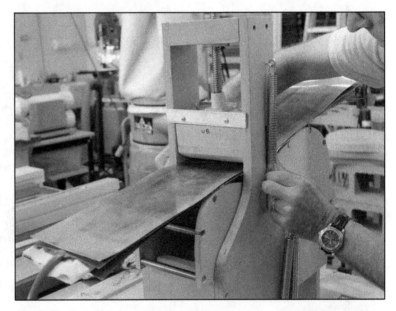

FIGURE 1.3.10. Once the heat blanket has gotten hot, the waist clamp is slowly screwed down all the way, and the upper and lower bout clamps are brought around to clamp the sides around the bouts. We will leave the side clamped in the bender until it cools. We will then reheat the side and wait until the sides are just cool enough to touch. We like to clamp the sides into the molds when they are still very warm and moist. After the sides are in the molds, they are left to dry, preferably a couple of days (if time permits).

FIGURE 1.3.11. Here is one side, clamped into the mold. In this photo, the overlap at the neck joint is being trimmed flush to the mold using a flush-trim saw. We will also trim the overlap at the other end, in preparation for putting the mold together.

FIGURE 1.3.12. This is a close-up of the freshly cut joint. Now it is time to put the two halves of the mold (and sides) together.

FIGURE 1.3.13. Here are the two sides being clamped together. Note there is a piece of wax paper between the ends of the sides and the mold. This is the case on both ends of the sides.

PREPARING AND GLUING THE ENDBLOCK AND HEADBLOCK

FIGURE 1.3.14. We are now going to shape the endblock and headblock, in preparation for gluing the sides together. The base of our jig that will sand the proper radius on the headblock is in the photo. This idea was borrowed from the shops of both Tom Ribbecke and Charles Fox. Many thanks to both Tom and Charles.

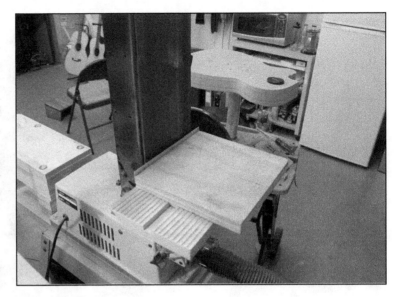

FIGURE 1.3.15. This is the other portion of the jig, the rotator. It will rest and rotate against the metal edge on the base. The radius of the rotator will match the radius of the end of the guitar, minus the distance from the sandpaper to the metal edge.

FIGURE 1.3.16. Here is the entire jig with an endblock blank tape with double-stick tape to the block on top of the jig. This block is rotated against the metal edge, and we'll sand the proper radius onto the endblock once the jig is properly set up.

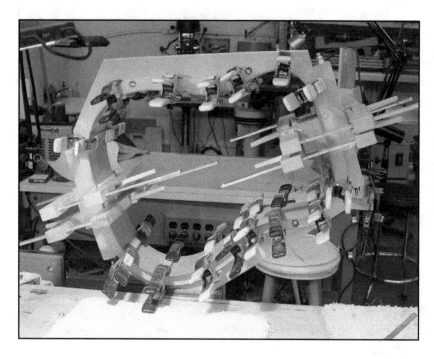

FIGURE 1.3.17. After we sand the proper radius on the endblock and headblock, they are glued and clamped to the sides.

FIGURE 1.3.18. While the blocks were being glued, we removed the clamps we had holding the sides to the mold and replaced them with go-bars. We have used this method for years to hold the sides in place while we are gluing on the kerf in the next step. Note that we don't take off all the clamps before putting on the go-bars. We only do a couple at a time to keep the sides exactly in place.

PROFILING THE SIDES

Note that we must be sure to use the proper hollow sanding discs in profiling the sides, because our top is a sphere with a 25' radius, and the back is a sphere with a 15' radius. When done correctly, the top and back plates will fit snugly into the properly profiled sides. The spherical radius on both the top and back will give them significantly more stiffness and strength than if they were to be left flat.

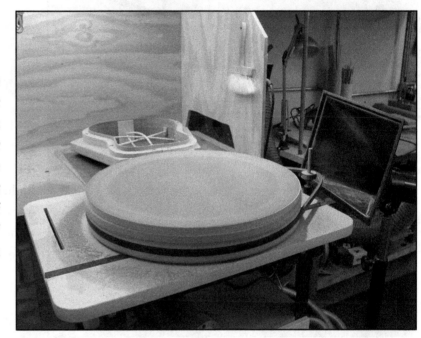

FIGURE 1.3.19. We use this is jig to sand down the sides to their proper profile. We got the idea for this jig from John Greven. Many thanks to John for his permission to show the jig here. We use different hollow form molds for the sanding surfaces. Since the back of the guitar has a 15' radius, we use a 15' hollow form, and for the top, we use a 25' form.

FIGURE 1.3.20. Here is the jig in use. It requires very little downward pressure to quickly sand away material, so much care must be used. Also, check each side often to be sure one side isn't getting shorter than the other. Also, we stop the jig when the sides are about 1/8" away from the mold. We don't want to damage the mold.

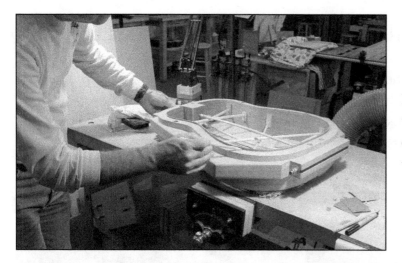

FIGURE 1.3.21. Once we've sanded to within about 1/8", we draw a line at the edge of the mold, which is at the height we want the sides to be.

FIGURE 1.3.22. Now we remove the screws holding on the mold ribs. With the ribs removed, we can put the sides back onto the sander and sand them down to the profile line.

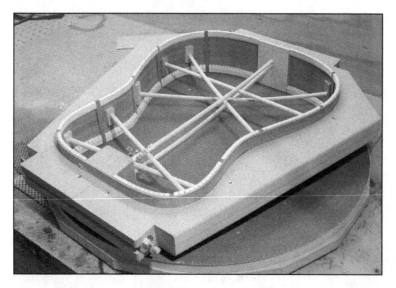

FIGURE 1.3.23. With the mold ribs removed, it is easy to install the kerf. We use reverse kerf on all our guitars with vertical "Popsicle" sticks every 4" to 6" for stability and to stop a crack if it starts in the side. The kerf is installed slightly high on the side, so it is 1/32" to 1/16" above the side when it is all glued in. For more detail on installing the kerf, see figures 2.1.68 and 2.1.69.

A brief word about the design of our molds: we designed this mold at the Phoenix Guitar Company. The core of the mold is similar to any other mold. However, the ribs are designed to have the exact profile of the sides of the guitar. We have used these molds for several years. Any time we have a new guitar to design, we first develop the mold with the proper radius on the top and back to properly match the guitar itself.

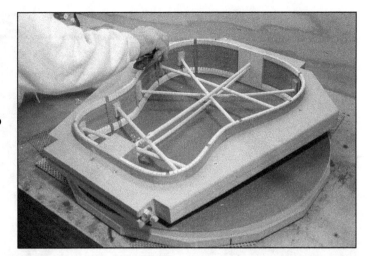

FIGURE 1.3.24. We use a small hand plane to remove the tallest areas of the kerf.

FIGURE 1.3.25. Now, we use the hollow mold forms to sand the kerf down to the level of the sides, endblock, and headblock. Remember to use the proper radius form—25′ for the top and 15′ for the back (in our case—many other guitar makers use different radii).

FITTING AND GLUING THE TOP AND BACK

FIGURE 1.3.26. With the sides and kerf profiled, we'll start fitting the top and back. First, we take the top and put the sides in position over it. The centerlines that were drawn on the endblock and headblock are aligned with the center seam on the top. Also, the tracing of the guitar shape, which was drawn on the underside of the top, must be aligned with the end of the headblock side of the guitar. This ensures that the distance between the head of the guitar and the sound hole is correct.

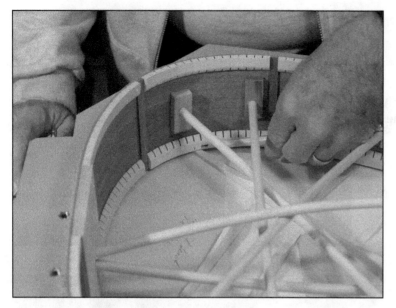

FIGURE 1.3.27. Each brace that crosses under the kerf must be marked at the point it touches the kerf. In addition, the kerf must be marked where the brace intersects it.

FIGURE 1.3.28. After marking the braces, the sides are moved, and we mark each brace 3/16″ outside the original mark. This is the thickness of the kerf. Then, as is shown in the photo, we will cut the brace down to the top wood. Take special care here; you don't want to damage the top.

FIGURE 1.3.29. Next, we use a chisel to remove the excess length of the brace. It must be cleaned right down to the top wood.

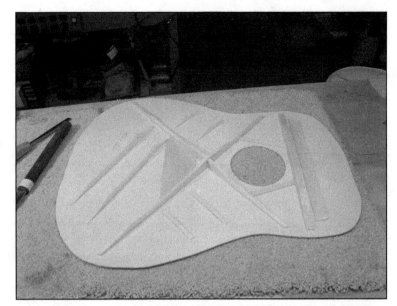

FIGURE 1.3.30. Here is the top, with all the braces trimmed.

FIGURE 1.3.31. Now we put the top away for a while and return to working on the sides. We will take the marks we made on the kerf sides and transfer them to the top of the kerf. Then, we use a straightedge and connect the edges consistent with the braces. In the photo, we are showing the mark one of the X braces will make on the kerf. Be sure to mark the correct brace angle. Once the marks are made, color them in with pencil to make them show.

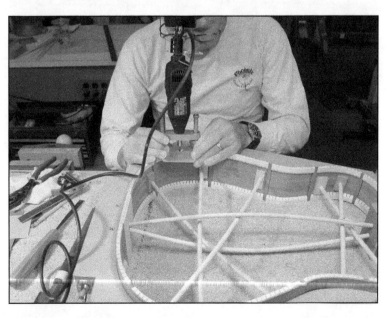

FIGURE 1.3.32. Now we will use a Dremel tool and carve a 1/8″ deep slot where we made the marks.

FIGURE 1.3.33. Here is a close-up of one of the slots. Once the top is put on, it will click right into position.

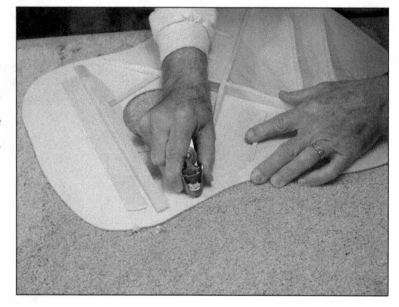

FIGURE 1.3.34. After fitting the top, any braces that are slightly over 1/8″ high at the ends must be planed down now or the top will not fit flush with the sides and kerf.

FIGURE 1.3.35. Here is a close-up of the top, showing where the braces are nicely tucked into their corresponding pockets.

FIGURE 1.3.36. Here, you can see the back braces have been fit to the kerf the same way as the top. We must now trim back the center strip. First, we mark it with a pencil on both ends.

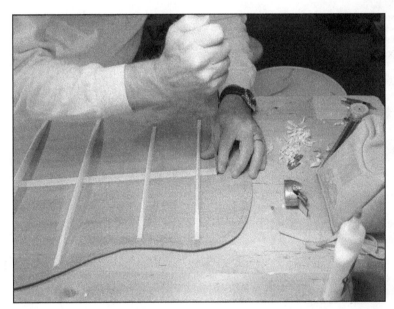

FIGURE 1.3.37. Using a sharp chisel, we cut the center strip, leaving the line so the fit to the headblock and endblock is tight, without any gaps. Then, erase any sign of the pencil line. Be sure to do this step on a hard surface and not on a carpeted surface. The downward pressure could split the back on a soft surface.

FIGURE 1.3.38. Now it's time to glue on the back. We glue the back first, since much of the back-to-kerf joint is visible through the sound hole. After clamping, we can clean this joint before gluing the top. In this photo, glue is being applied to the kerf.

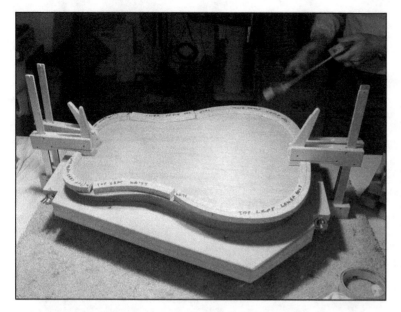

FIGURE 1.3.39. After we make sure all the braces are properly tucked into their pockets in the kerf, we apply clamps to each end of the guitar, directly onto the endblock and headblock. Then, we put cauls around the perimeter of the guitar, directly over the guitar sides.

FIGURE 1.3.40. Now clamps are put around the guitar, using the cauls for even pressure distribution.

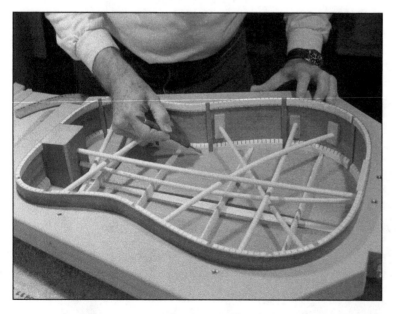

FIGURE 1.3.41. Once the glue is dry, we remove the clamps, turn the box over, and clean up any glue that has squeezed out.

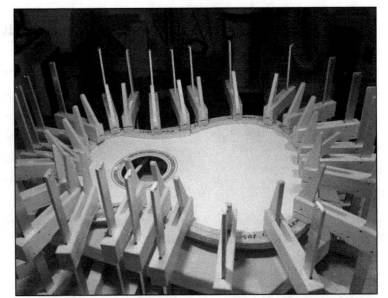

FIGURE 1.3.42. Now, we glue the top in the same way that we did the back.

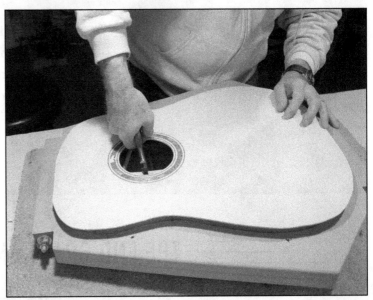

FIGURE 1.3.43. After the glue dries, we must remove the go-bars before the box is removed from the mold. The long go-bars between the endblock and headblock must be cut with nippers. The rest can be removed simply by pulling them out.

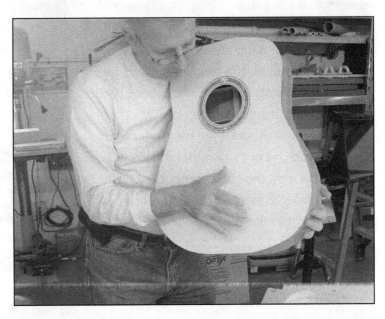

FIGURE 1.3.44. Once the guitar body is removed from the mold, we always tap the body to hear its response. A large body guitar like this should have a deep, clear ring. If the tap tone is muffled, like it's stuffed with a pillow, you have a serious problem. You will probably have to saw off the top and make another one, because the instrument will not have a good sound.

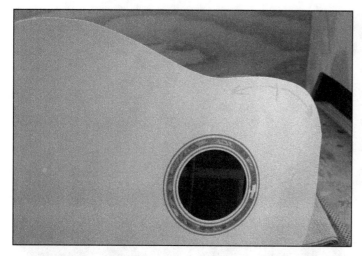

FIGURE 1.3.45. We are now ready to remove the top and back overhang. The marks drawn on the top show the direction we need to move the router to avoid cracks. You must start routing at the peaks of the upper and lower bouts, moving the router toward the waist and around to the headblock and tailblock. The direction you move the router is very important. If you move the router in the wrong direction, you risk creating a split in the top that likely can't be fixed.

FIGURE 1.3.46. Here is a photo of the first cut made with the flush-trim laminate trimmer shown. After the sections are complete for the top and back, we are ready to install the end graft.

THE END GRAFT AND BINDINGS

FIGURE 1.3.47. After the top and back overhangs are trimmed, the guitar is placed into a fixture we have on our benches to hold bodies while they are being worked on—two clamps, placed far enough apart for the upper bout to pass between but not so far that the lower bout passes. This way, the guitar cannot fall through and be damaged. We pad the guitar body with shop rags and make sure it is secure.

FIGURE 1.3.48. Now we are ready to make the end graft. First, we select a piece of Indian rosewood and cut it on the band saw to the approximate shape, only oversized. We place it in the first clamp-down of the jig, and one edge is cut clean on the table saw. This jig was the idea of Charles Fox. We want to thank Charles for permission to show the jig.

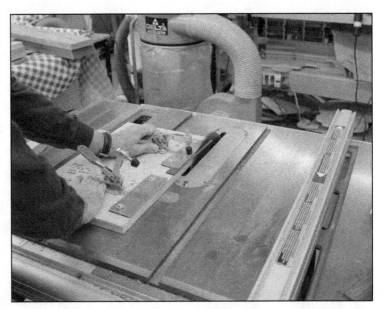

FIGURE 1.3.49. Here is the second part of the jig. After making the first cut, the graft is turned so that the freshly cut side is put inside, against the jig edge, and the rough side is outside, ready to be cut on the jig. You can see the rough sliver being cut off.

FIGURE 1.3.50. Here is the final graft. Note the grain is lengthwise on the graft. This will make it stand out and look better when it is inlaid.

FIGURE 1.3.51. This jig enables us to accurately cut the channel for the end graft into the guitar body. The top of the jig is 3/8″ plexiglass, and with the wing screws (which are also on the other side), we can tighten the jig onto any of our guitar sizes. Again, thanks to Charles Fox for the idea for this jig.

FIGURE 1.3.52. For the cut, we use a small plunge router with a collar screwed into the base. A 1/4″ spiral bit makes the actual cut.

FIGURE 1.3.53. The depth of cut is set to go just through the thickness of the side and is checked with a quick cut just to be sure. At this point, we can still change the depth if necessary.

FIGURE 1.3.54. The collar on the router base follows the edge of the jig. It is important to bring the cutter into the guitar top and back rather than to start in the middle of the pattern and push the cutter out. This will help avoid tear-out on the top and back.

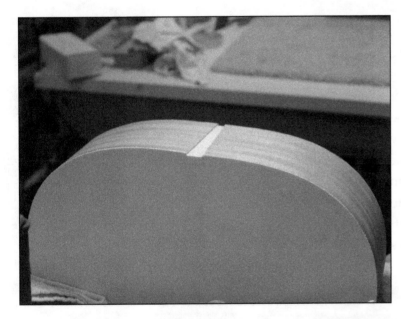

FIGURE 1.3.55. Here is the final cut. The depth of the cut should always be slightly less than the thickness of the graft. You want the graft to be a little higher than the side when it is glued in. Otherwise, you have a low graft and a low spot in the side or have to put a shim under the graft to bring its level up.

FIGURE 1.3.56. Here is the graft with a piece of b/w/b purfling on each side of the Indian rosewood piece.

FIGURE 1.3.57. After trimming the ends of the graft, we use a cabinet scraper to level the graft with the sides.

FIGURE 1.3.58. Now, we will level the sides. One method we will use is gently moving the guitar around the sides on a belt sander. We always use either 220- or 320-grit sandpaper for this job because it is very easy to sand too aggressively. In addition, we never put the body down on the sander while it is moving. We use a foot switch. We will put the guitar in position and activate the switch when we are ready to sand. Then we turn the sander off when we lift the body off the sander. Also, *always* keep the guitar moving when using this method. Otherwise, it is easy to create a flat spot.

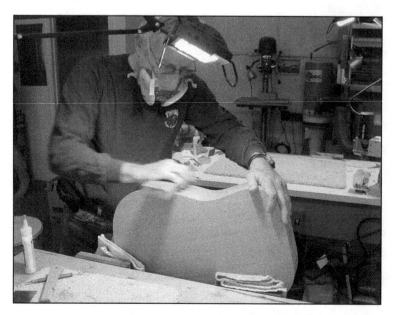

FIGURE 1.3.59. After using the belt sander, we will continue sanding with a block with sandpaper glued to it. We don't try to do all final sanding with the belt—it's just too aggressive, and we prefer to final sand with blocks. This flat block is great for convex rounded edges.

FIGURE 1.3.60. For the waist, we use a thick dowel (about 1 1/4") with self-stick sandpaper attached. Note that in each of the photos, a dust mask is used during the sanding process. Sanding creates a lot of very fine dust, and you need to protect your lungs. We also have an overhead dust collector on the ceiling to help reduce the airborne dust. Also note that we continue to use the same bench clamping fixture to hold the body that we used when cutting the end graft. As long as the body is put in from the top, it can't fall through (and *never* put the guitar in from the bottom).

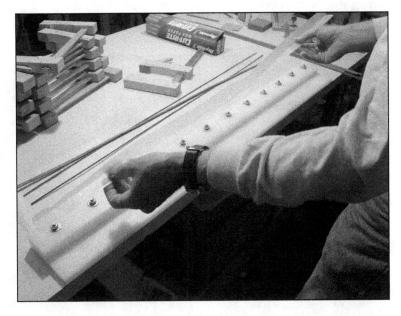

FIGURE 1.3.61. With the body sanded, it is time to prepare the bindings. We start with a jig we created that is made of ultra-high-density polyethylene. It simply creates a shelf to clamp the bindings against. Though this material is used to eliminate as much glue sticking to it as possible, unfortunately, it still does stick, so we have cut a piece of wax paper about 36" long and 1" wide and fold it lengthwise to fit against the wall of the jig.

FIGURE 1.3.62. In this photo, you can see the Indian rosewood binding (sanded flat on one edge) being clamped against a strip of b/w/b purfling by a series of small wedges between the cam clamps and the jig. We will push both the binding and purfling down solidly against the bottom of the jig using a small flat-blade screwdriver.

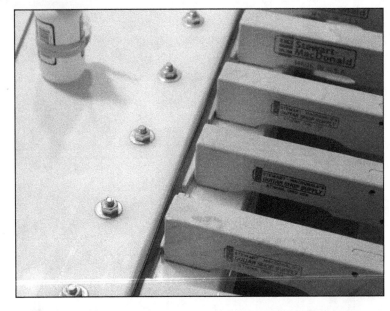

FIGURE 1.3.63. Once we're happy that the bindings and purflings are solidly down against the base of the jig, we will use a small pipette filled with superglue to run a bead of superglue between the binding and the purfling. Use the very thin superglue, and it will have no problem seeping between the clamped binding and purfling to form a good glue joint. Note: *do not* use superglue if you are using light bindings (like maple). Superglue can stain the very light woods yellow, and the stain will not sand out. If you use lighter woods, it's best to use epoxy for the glue step, then clamp the bindings and purflings together after gluing. You do not want to use regular wood glue, because we are going to put the bindings into a hot bender, and we don't want the glue joint to come apart.

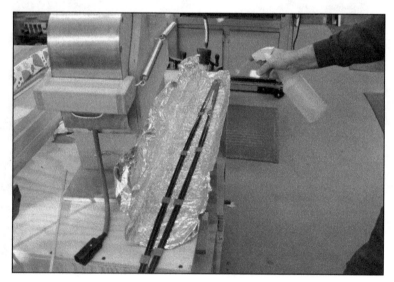

FIGURE 1.3.64. Now, we mark the waist of the bindings, just as we did on the sides (we kept the original masking tape on the edge of one of our benches). Then we wet them with water and put them into the bender.

FIGURE 1.3.65. As the bindings are cooling, it's time to cut the binding and purfling slots in the body. We are using the LMI binding jig (originally designed by Tom Ribbecke), and first we must be sure the body sides are perpendicular to the table.

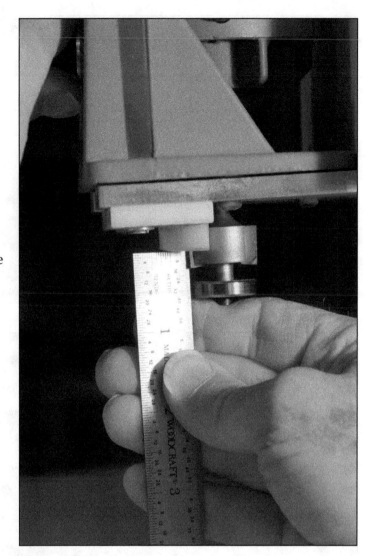

FIGURE 1.3.66. The depth of cut is critical, so we are measuring the depth of the binding cut.

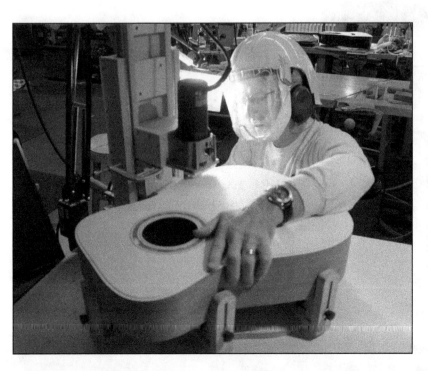

FIGURE 1.3.67. In this photo, the purfling cut has already been made, and we are making the binding cut. With this jig, we only have to change the bearing size and depth of cut to change between the different cuts, since the router (or laminate trimmer) is always held vertically.

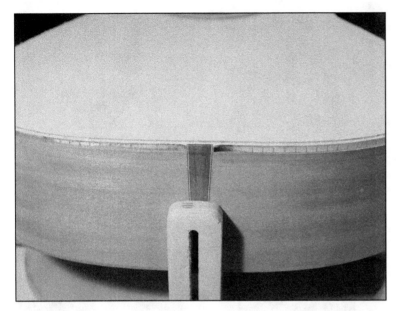

FIGURE 1.3.68. If you plan to miter your purflings around the end graft, you have to stop the binding cuts before they get to the end graft. We will show the steps for mitering the purflings.

FIGURE 1.3.69. The curved section created by the bit diameter must be cleaned out with a chisel. First, use the flat part of the blade to extend the flat portion of the binding cut up to the end graft purfling.

FIGURE 1.3.70. Next, put the chisel blade directly in the binding slot and clean out the necessary wood.

FIGURE 1.3.71. This photo shows how the ends of the end graft are trimmed by taping a piece of purfling against the guitar top (and back) and rerunning the binding cut. This will trim the end graft exactly the thickness of the purfling higher than the original binding cut.

FIGURE 1.3.72. Here is the guitar body, with all the bindings bent and ready to go.

FIGURE 1.3.73. Each piece of binding is held up to the guitar, and we mark the guitar side and the binding so we can find the proper alignment. We make the mark at the waist.

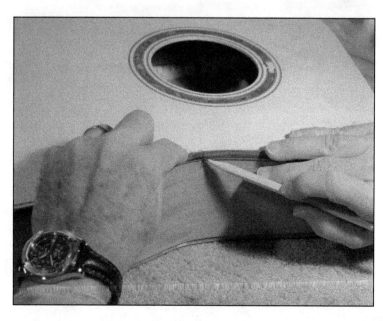

FIGURE 1.3.74. With the binding line aligned with the line on the side of the guitar, we bring the binding around to the end graft and mark the center. We will repeat this operation with the bindings on the other side and the back.

FIGURE 1.3.75. Once both topside bindings are marked, they are held together and the ends are sanded down to the marks (maybe shy by just a teeny little bit).

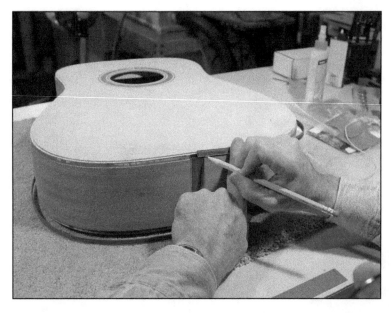

FIGURE 1.3.76. Now we put each binding back onto its respective binding slot and mark where the purfling will be mitered with the purfling of the end graft.

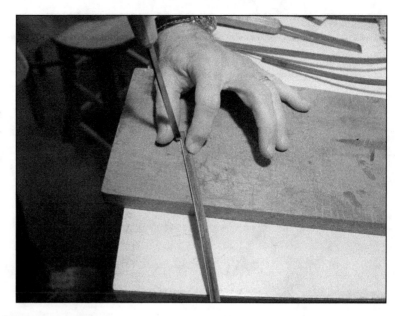

FIGURE 1.3.77. Now the purfling on the bottom edge of the binding is cut at nearly a 45-degree angle at the point where the end graft purfling meets the end graft purfling.

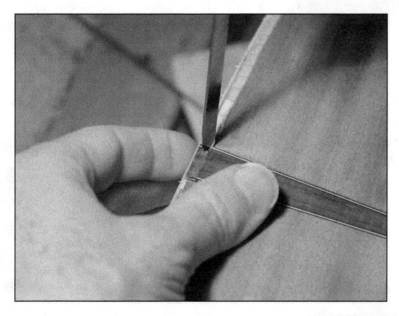

FIGURE 1.3.78. We trim the purfling edge of the endgraft to about a 45-degree angle. It may be just slightly different than an actual 45-degree angle, but not much. The angle is not as important as making the ends match each other.

FIGURE 1.3.79. After a little fitting between the edges of the purfling angles and the ends of the bindings and after sanding on the disc sander, we make all the edges line up.

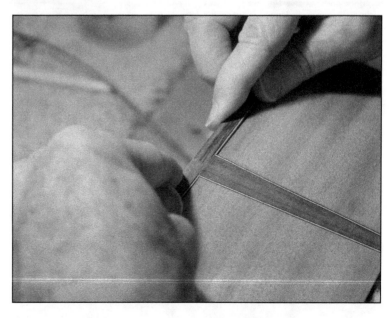

FIGURE 1.3.80. Now we must prepare the purflings that will go on the top of the guitar. First, we have to use a sharp chisel to miter the edges of the purflings so the right and left sides match up perfectly.

FIGURE 1.3.81. Once the purflings line up properly, they, along with the binding strip are taped to the guitar, in their proper positions. A piece of masking tape will do.

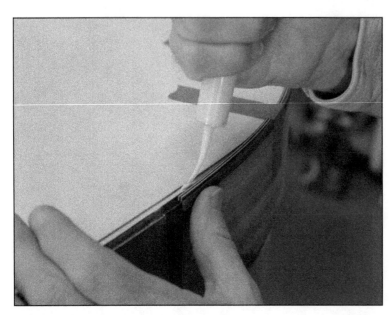

FIGURE 1.3.82. Glue is now squeezed between all the purflings and binding. We use a plastic syringe filled with Titebond for the job.

FIGURE 1.3.83. We will typically glue for a few inches, then bind the glued area with the flat nylon rope and repeat the process, gluing a few inches and then binding.

FIGURE 1.3.84. Here is the first piece of binding, all strapped down. After this piece of binding, we will put on the other piece of the top binding, then turn the guitar body over and do each side of the back binding.

FIGURE 1.3.85. Here are all four pieces of binding, all strapped down. Note how we use a cam clamp to tie down the end of the nylon rope. Now for the details up at the neck end.

FIGURE 1.3.86. On the top of the guitar, at the headblock end, the bindings and purflings do not need to be carefully mitered because they are hidden under the fingerboard. However, they need to be mitered on the back of the guitar because the joint is clearly visible. We will start by only gluing the binding and purfling to within about 4″ or so of the center joint. This leaves us plenty of free space to manipulate the binding and purfling. We have left plenty of overlap.

FIGURE 1.3.87. We are marking the centerline for each of the overlapping bindings on the guitar back. Note the binding at the top has a gap. This is no problem. The fingerboard hides this area, but it will be cut away when we cut the dovetail. We have to pay attention to the joint at the back of the guitar.

FIGURE 1.3.88. Here we are cutting most of the binding overlap away. We will only leave between 1/32″ and 1/16″. We put a piece of scrap wood under the binding so the guitar isn't cut.

FIGURE 1.3.89. Now we will focus on the purfling. First, we mark the centerline on each piece.

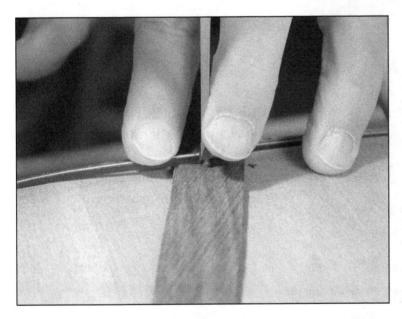

FIGURE 1.3.90. Now, one at a time, each purfling piece is bent over the guitar back, where it can be worked on, and we put a piece of scrap under it. A sharp chisel is used to nip away the excess, a little at a time. Note that this is done right over the headblock, so there is a very stable block of wood under all the work being done.

FIGURE 1.3.91. As the fit gets close while you are using the chisel, you may want to change to a sanding block to have more control. Do this on each side, checking the fit often, until the two pieces of purfling make a perfect fit.

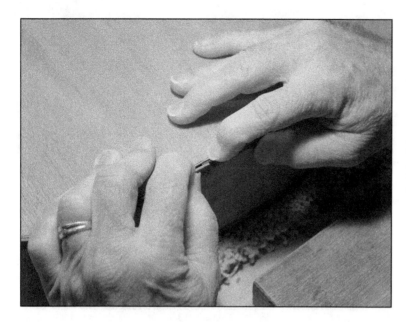

FIGURE 1.3.92. Here is the completed purfling. Now it's time to get the binding done.

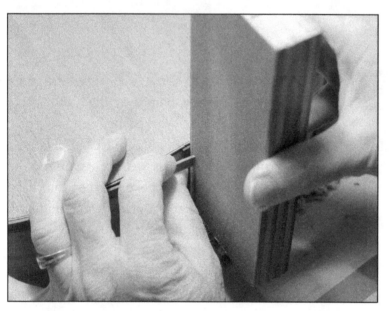

FIGURE 1.3.93. At this point, if the binding overlap is too much, it can be trimmed with the saw as before. Once it is close, we like to use a block sander to finalize the binding on both sides until the fit is just right.

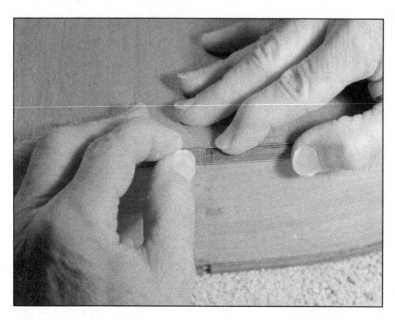

FIGURE 1.3.94. Here is the final binding fit. Time to glue everything down.

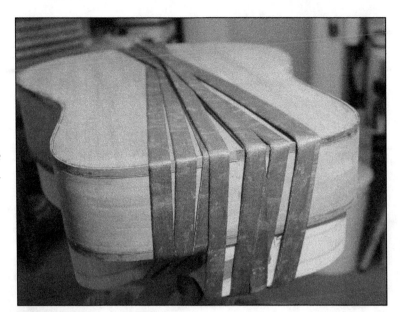

FIGURE 1.3.95. Here is the glue-up of the back binding and purfling around the shoulders and headblock of the guitar.

FIGURE 1.3.96. Time to scrape and sand the bindings down.

FIGURE 1.3.97. After scraping, sanding, and leveling all the bindings and purflings, the body is ready for the dovetail to be cut.

FIGURE 1.3.98. Here is our jig for cutting a dovetail. This view shows the body being held in place.

FIGURE1.3.99. Here is the top view of the jig, with the guitar body ready for the next step. The plexiglass template we use is a dovetail template from Stewart MacDonald. The guitar body depth measures just over 3″ deep at this point, so we are going to set the dovetail to cut 2 3/4″ down from the guitar top, with a 3/4″ depth of cut. We'll have to remember these important dimensions later.

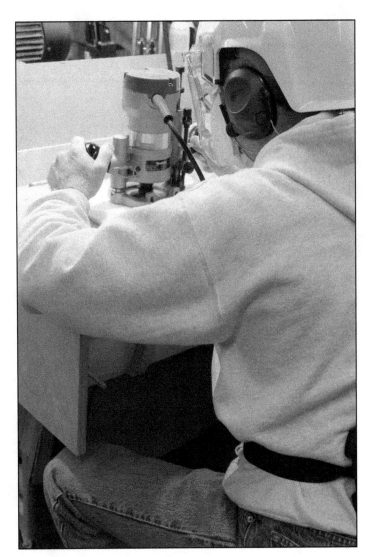

FIGURE1.3.100. We are making the dovetail cut.

FIGURE 1.3.10.1. This is the final dovetail cut. At this point, we are finished with the guitar body. After only a small amount of final sanding, the body will be ready for finish.

1.4
THE STEEL STRING NECK

In this chapter, we will cover how we make our necks, from basic glue-up to shaping, carving, inlay, fingerboard preparation and gluing, and fitting the neck to the body.

NECK GLUE-UP

FIGURE 1.4.1. With our guitars, the steel string neck starts out very much like our archtop or classical necks. The main difference between any of the necks is the scale length and the neck width. Almost all our necks are a five-piece sandwich. The neck is three pieces of mahogany separated by veneers of walnut. If the mahogany slabs we have in stock are slightly too thin for the proper neck width at its widest point (the fourteenth fret for a steel string or archtop and the twelfth fret for a classical), then we have a choice: either get wider pieces of mahogany or resaw off wider slabs of walnut to make the proper width neck instead of using veneers of walnut. We like the neck at its widest to be at least 1/16" oversize, just to be safe. In this photo, you can see a nice board of African mahogany being resawn, which will be the two outer sides and will make four necks. Also note that the grain is in the vertical or quartersawn direction.

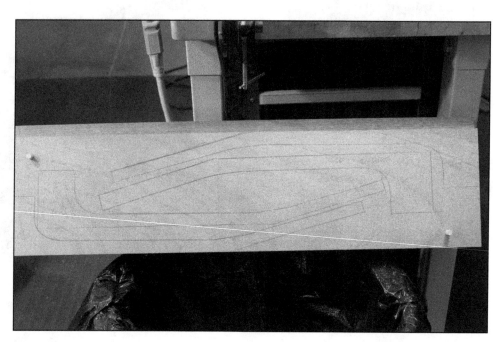

FIGURE 1.4.2. Here is the sandwich, ready for gluing. Note the two dowels in the corners for alignment. These will keep the boards from slipping during the clamping process.

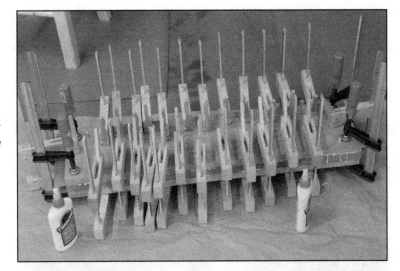

FIGURE 1.4.3. Here is the glue-up. We will typically wait twenty-four hours before the next step.

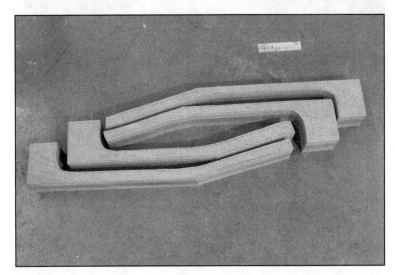

FIGURE 1.4.4. After drying, we will use a band saw to separate the necks.

INITIAL NECK SHAPING

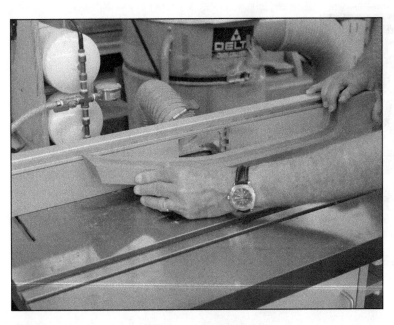

FIGURE 1.4.5. After the boards have been sawn apart, we will remove the neck intended for this guitar and joint the fingerboard side of the neck. Next, we will use a 1/4″ router bit and cut the truss rod slot into the neck. For this step, we use a router table, but we've seen many luthiers choose to use a table saw for this step instead.

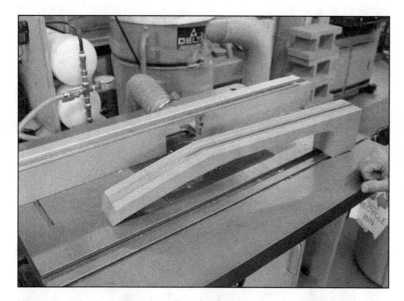

FIGURE 1.4.6. Here is the completed truss rod slot. All our truss rods are two-way rods and are 3/8″ tall. We make a slot about 1/32″ deeper than the rod itself.

FIGURE 1.4.7. Since the neck is rough-cut from the glued board, the headstock angle is not accurate. The jig shown will let us properly flatten the headstock and make its angle an exact 15 degrees. Thanks to Tom Ribbecke for this idea.

FIGURE 1.4.8. Here is the neck, clamped into the angle jig. You can see that we have to remove about 1/8″ of wood to get the top of the headstock flat. We will do this in very small passes (maybe 1/64″ per pass to reduce tear-out).

FIGURE 1.4.9. We always put the headstock into the jointer at an angle, since we're cutting into end grain. As we cut, we straighten out the headstock so that it completes the cut at a 90-degree angle to the wood. We also have a helical cutter on our jointer (multiple small heads, arranged in a spiral pattern). This makes this kind of cut much safer than a simple straight-blade jointer.

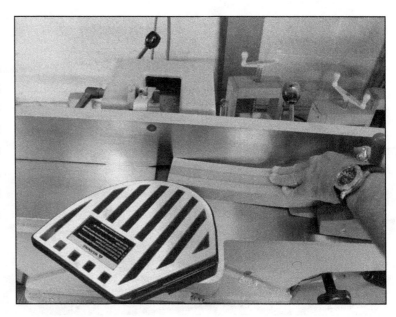

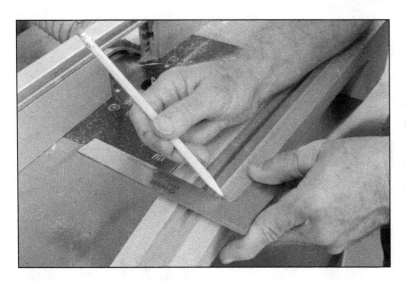

FIGURE 1.4.10. After the cut is complete, check to make sure that the edge of the angle is perpendicular to the edge of the neck. We pencil in this edge, since it will mark the edge of the fingerboard.

FIGURE 1.4.11. Next, we use a 6 mm metric bit to cut the slots for the carbon fiber rods. We put these rods as stiffeners on all our steel string and archtop guitars. They add very little weight but add a lot in strength. The rods are 5 mm wide and 1/4" deep, so a 5-mm cut is too small. We make this cut from about 1/4" from the nut to about the fourteenth fret. This is not necessarily a requirement for a steel string neck. Many manufacturers only use a truss rod; however, we have chosen to use the carbon fiber rods for our production guitars because of the additional stiffness and strength they offer.

FIGURE 1.4.12. Here is a photo of the jig we use to do the initial cut on our necks to give them their approximate thickness. We also use it to shape the volute in the neck.

FIGURE 1.4.13. Here is the rough neck clamped into the jig. It cuts about 1/32" thicker than our ideal final dimension to give us some slack for final shaping and sanding. We have made several of these neck-shaping jigs for different scale lengths, twelve- versus fourteen-fret necks, etc. Ideally, we would have one for every size and type neck we make. Instead, we have them for our most popular sizes. If someone orders something we consider a one-off, we may not make a special jig, since everything takes up space in the shop.

FINGERBOARD PREPARATION

Before continuing with the neck, we have to get the fingerboard ready.

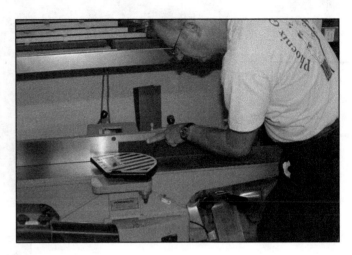

FIGURE 1.4.14. To prepare the fingerboard, we will start with a rough ebony board about 3″ wide, and thickness-sand it down to slightly over 1/4″ thick (about 1/64″ over). Then we joint one edge, nice and level.

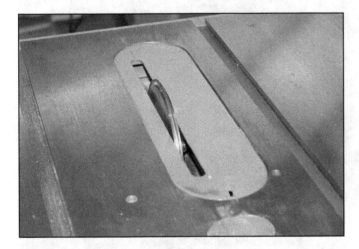

FIGURE 1.4.15. Next, be sure the saw blade has been replaced with a fretting blade (kerf 0.022″). Note that the blade has a couple of steel stiffeners on each side of the blade. They are there to keep the blade from drifting during the cut.

FIGURE 1.4.16. After the blade is in place, we put our sled onto the saw and measure the height of the blade above the sled table. This is how deep the blade will cut into the fingerboard. Ideally, it will cut at least halfway through the board, maybe just a little more. After we've made a measurement, we will try a test cut with a piece of scrap. Once we're happy with the depth of cut, it's time to actually cut the fret slots. Notice our fingerboard has been taped to our slotting template with double-sided tape. The jointed edge is perfectly aligned with the edge of the template being used for the fret slot measurements. In this case, it's a 25.31″ scale length, and the 25.31″ slotting template is the one on the right side of the template.

FIGURE 1.4.17. Here is the completed board. Notice the pin in the sled. It is used to fit into each slot in the template to properly guide the fingerboard over the saw blade. Ideally, we just run each slot through the blade in one direction. If you go through and back, the slot is very slightly widened. This can cause the fret to not sit quite as well in the slot, particularly at the fret ends.

FIGURE 1.4.18. To remove the fingerboard from the template, use some naphtha in a pipette and carefully lift the board with a thin knife edge. We use an artist's pallet knife for this. You must be patient and let the naphtha do its job loosening the tape. If you force it, you could crack the fingerboard—particularly at a fret slot.

FIGURE 1.4.19. A centerline must now be drawn onto the fingerboard using a right angle from the good, straight-jointed edge. Since this is the side of the board that is perpendicular to the fret slots, the center-line must be parallel to this side. Draw the centerline on one side, then transfer it to the other side so it is visible on both the top and back of the board.

FIGURE 1.4.20. We now have to prepare the fingerboard bindings to complete the fingerboard. We are using Indian rosewood for the bindings for the steel string and Macassar ebony for the archtop and the classical, all with a thin veneer (approximately 0.020) of maple separating the bindings from the fingerboard. Since the next several steps are identical, we will only show them once. The photo shows us cutting binding strips from a board on the band saw.

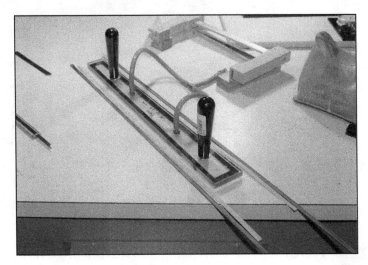

FIGURE 1.4.21. Here are the binding and purfling strips, along with a vacuum template we made. The template will hold the fingerboard, and a flush-trim router bit will ride the edge of the template to trim the fingerboard to the exact size. Now, we must make sure that the template plus the width of the binding and purfling equals the final fingerboard width desired.

FIGURE 1.4.22. Here is the template with both bindings and both maple purflings being measured. At this point, if the measurement is too large (and we typically start with very thick bindings to make sure the measurement is too large), we have two choices. First, we can put the bindings through the thickness sander to reduce their thickness. Second, we can joint very small amounts from each side of the fingerboard (you must joint both sides). Our template was made to make the fingerboard come out at exactly 1 3/4" at the nut, using two 0.020 purflings, and two 0.080 bindings. From our experience, it's much easier to sand off very slight amounts from the bindings than to joint off the same very small amounts from the fingerboard.

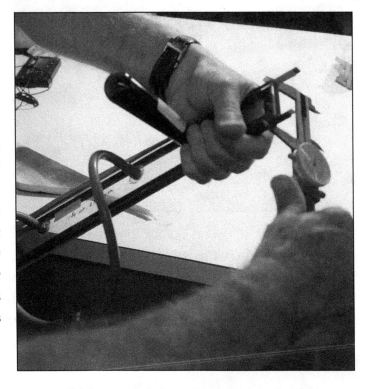

FIGURE 1.4.23. After the proper measurement has been reached, (in this case, through sizing of the bindings), the template is placed on the fingerboard and is drawn. Then we band saw the fingerboard shape, which is oversize by about 1/16″.

FIGURE 1.4.24. This is a photo of our vacuum jig. It was built using plans from joewoodworker.com. It works extremely well, and such a system is almost critical in any small shop.

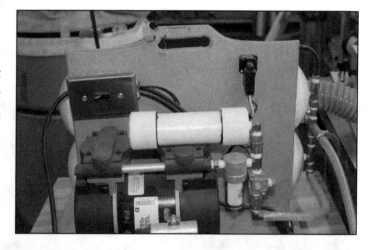

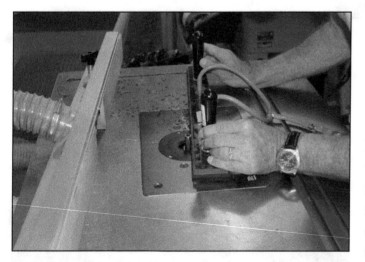

FIGURE 1.4.25. The fingerboard blank is now placed onto the vacuum template, shown above, with the fret slots down. The centerline on the fingerboard is aligned with the centerline drawn onto the vacuum template. We use a spiral, flush-cut bit used for this step. In addition, you absolutely must know the direction of your grain, as the router bit is cutting it. In the case of ebony, it is often difficult to tell what direction the grain is running, so we recommend what we call nibble cuts to do this step. We will start the cutting toward the far right side of the board and make a cut of about 1/4″ (going against the direction of the spin of the bit). We will then repeat this procedure every 1/8″ to 1/4″ as we slowly cut toward the left side of the board. We have had cases where the grain has run out, and the bit has been able to dig directly into end grain and caused a tear-out instead of a clean cut. However, by using this nibble-cut method, we haven't had a problem. If you don't have vacuum capability in your shop, you can use double-sided tape to hold your fingerboard to the jig. Just be sure to put good handles on the jig. Keep your fingers away from the blade!

FIGURE 1.4.26. After both sides of the fingerboard are routed smooth, sand the board smooth on a disc sander at the twenty-second fret (assuming you have a twenty-one-fret fingerboard). The nut side of the fingerboard can be left alone for a while.

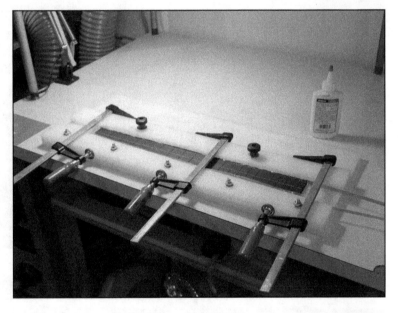

FIGURE 1.4.27. As shown in the photo, we have built a jig out of UHDP (ultra-high-density polyethylene) to glue our purfling and bindings to the fingerboard. We use a small screwdriver blade to push the maple purfling down so it doesn't creep up. In addition, we will cut a couple of 1" wide pieces of wax paper to go around the glue-up to keep glue out of the jig.

FIGURE 1.4.28. After the purfling is glued, use a fretting saw to cut fret slots into the purfling. We like to use a pull stroke for this job so we don't get tear-out or risk pulling the maple away from the ebony fingerboard.

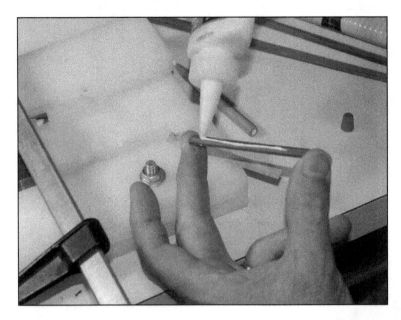

FIGURE 1.4.29. While the bindings are being glued to the fingerboard in the jig, glue a small piece of binding to a piece of maple purfling (long enough to go over the end of the fingerboard.

FIGURE 1.4.30. After the bindings have been glued to the fingerboard, cut them to within about 1/8″ from the end of the fingerboard and use a chisel to cut a 45-degree miter cut.

FIGURE 1.4.31. Here is the final miter.

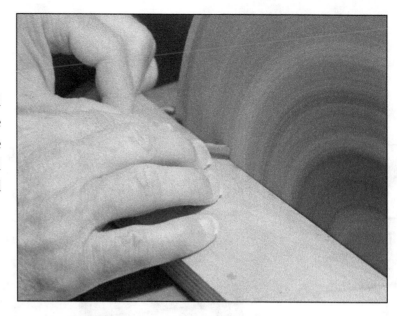

FIGURE 1.4.32. Now we take the small glue-up of the binding and purfling and use a disc sander to put the miter angle on the fingerboard end cap. Check the fit often and keep working the angle of the end cap until it is right. Then do the other side of the cap.

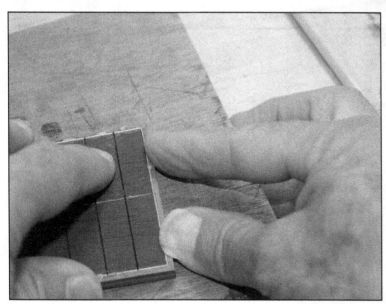

FIG, 1.4.33. Here is the final fit of the fingerboard end cap. We haven't yet worried about cleaning up the glue. That will happen automatically in a little while.

FIGURE 1.4.34. At this point, we clamp the fingerboard to a bench top with a small piece of wax paper under the end of the fingerboard. We use a couple of cam clamps as shown very close to the end of the board. Then, we glue the fingerboard end cap to the fingerboard. Two very small wedges are pushed into the gap between the cam clamps and the end cap to apply the proper clamping pressure to the glue-up.

FIGURE 1.4.35. The fingerboard is secured with double-sided tape to the underside of our radius jig. Care must be taken to be sure the centerline on the fingerboard is properly aligned to the centerline on the jig. Also, be sure the back side of the fingerboard is taped to the jig. It would be a shame to sand the radius onto the wrong side of the fingerboard.

FIGURE 1.4.36. Here is a photo of the end of the fingerboard, just before we sand the radius.

FIGURE 1.4.37. Here is the jig in use. While the fingerboard is being sanded, the jig is gently rocked back and forth until the radius is complete. If you attempt to build a jig like this, try it with scrap fingerboards first until you have the hang of it.

Note that for each of the guitars we are writing about in this book, we have different radii on the fingerboard. The archtop has a 12″ radius (by customer request), the steel string has a 16″ radius (our standard), and the classical has a 20″ radius (again, our standard).

FIGURE 1.4.38. Here is the fingerboard with the radius sanded.

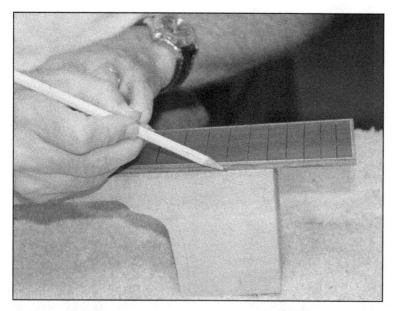

FIGURE 1.4.39. Once the fingerboard is done, it is placed onto the neck blank. The nut end of the fingerboard is placed onto the break line of the headstock, and a pencil is used to mark the fifteenth fret. We mark the fifteenth fret because this is the end of the dovetail. The dovetail is exactly 5/8″ long, which also happens to be the same distance from the fourteenth to the fifteenth fret. Now, use a band saw to saw the fingerboard off at the fifteenth fret mark—at the proper angle for the neck. It is important to note that we have the nut edge of the fingerboard exactly on the angled edge of the headstock. This way, the nut of the guitar is actually on the angled headstock. Some luthiers move their fingerboards forward so the nut is not on the headstock—either method is OK.

CUTTING THE DOVETAIL

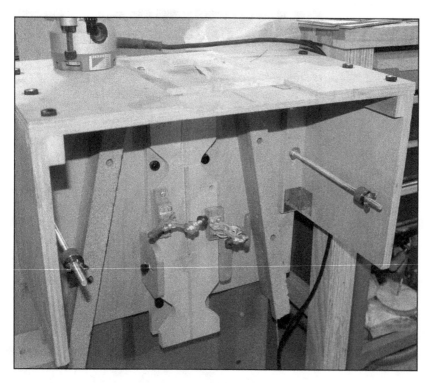

FIGURE 1.4.40. This is the jig that we use for cutting dovetails (thanks to Tom Ribbecke for this idea). The truss rod slot fits into the 1/4″ extension in the center of the vertical board and is clamped into place using the two clamps. The hinge at the top of the board allows the angle of the cut to be easily changed, depending on the type of guitar we are making. For the steel string, the angle will be approximately 2 degrees. For an archtop, the angle is approximately 4 degrees, matching the angle of the end of the dovetail above.

 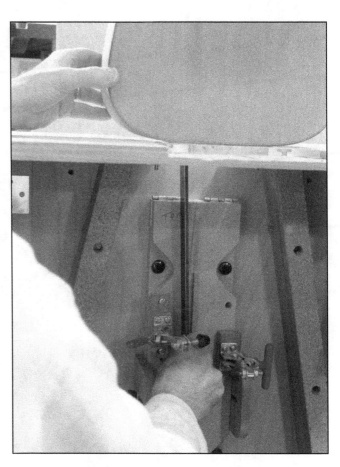

FIG 1.4.41 AND 1.4.42. In the two photos above, a straightedge is placed on the moveable, tilting surface of the fingerboard dovetail jig as the guitar body sits on the top of the jig. Once the straightedge is level over the upper body of the guitar, the neck angle is correct. This makes finding the neck angle very easy for our steel string and standard classical guitars. The classical guitar being shown in this book will use a raised fingerboard, so it will have a different method of finding the neck angle—as does the archtop. In these cases, a drawing must be used to determine the proper angle.

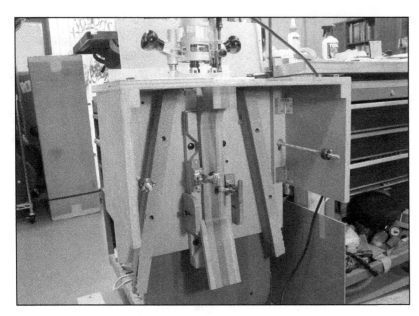

FIGURE 1.4.43. Here is the neck clamped into the dovetail jig after the proper angle from the step above was determined.

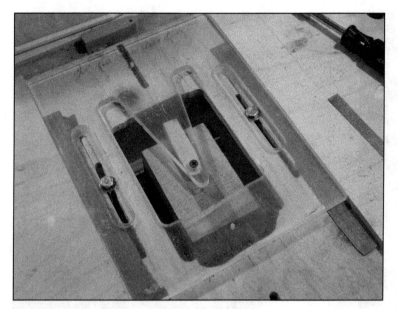

FIGURE 1.4.44. Here is the top view of the neck in the jig. In addition to the clamps, the neck is screwed to the template, so it is secured very well. The template is from Stewart MacDonald.

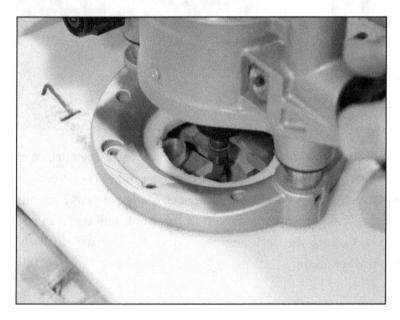

FIGURE 1.4.45. Here is the router bit making the dovetail cut in the neck. The template extends approximately 1/4" less down the neck heel versus the cut in the body (remember, the dovetail cut in the body extends 2 3/4"), and the depth of the cut is 5/8".

There is a reason that the dovetail cut in the neck is 1/8" shorter than the cut in the body, resulting in a 1/8" gap between the end of the neck dovetail and the body dovetail. For those of you who have removed dovetail necks to do repairs, like neck resets, the common procedure is to remove the fifteenth fret and drill a couple of small holes into the fret slot through the fingerboard into that gap discussed above. Then steam is injected into the gap by using a cappuccino machine and blowing the steam through a basketball nozzle. If above the gap doesn't exist or doesn't line up with the fifteenth fret, it becomes difficult or impossible to inject steam into the glue joint to remove the neck. You should always make your guitars so they can be repaired.

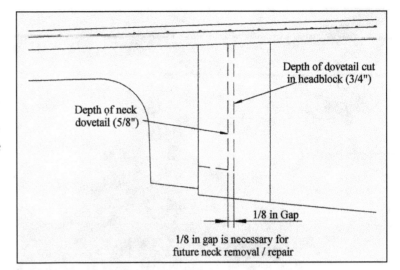

DRAWING 1.4.1. The Dovetail Profile. Note the fifteenth fret is directly above the 1/8″ gap.

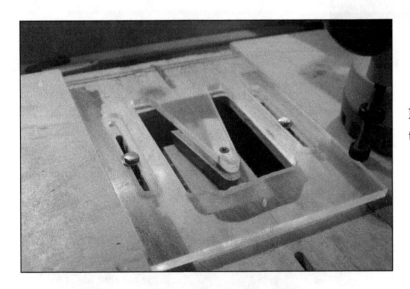

FIGURE 1.4.46. Here is the final dovetail for the neck. The depth of this cut is 5/8″.

THE HEADSTOCK "EARS," SHAPING THE HEEL, AND GLUING THE CARBON FIBER RODS

FIGURE 1.4.47. After cutting the dovetail, we glue the ears onto the headstock. We will try to use some cutoff pieces from the same neck block that the neck came from so the ears will match as closely as possible to the neck itself.

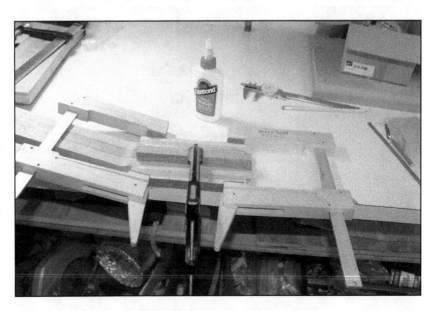

FIGURE 1.4.48. We are marking the position of the fingerboard on the neck. Each fingerboard edge is measured and marked to be equidistant from the edges of the neck.

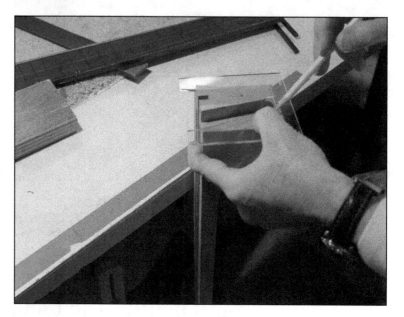

FIGURE 1.4.49. We are using a plexiglass template showing the shape of our neck heel. We will use this shape as we carve the heel.

FIGURE 1.4.50. We use our large belt sander to carve away the excess material and get the final heel shape.

FIGURE 1.4.51. Here is the carved heel (slightly oversize). You can see that the outer drawing is the template tracing made above. The inner line is the point where we will carve away a shelf from the line up to the dovetail. This means we only have a thin shelf to meet the guitar side as the neck is fit. It would be a much more difficult fit if the entire flat area needed to be fit to the guitar sides.

FIGURE 1.4.52. Here is the heel with the shelf carved out. It is about 1/32″ deep. As the final neck carve is done, the dimension will approach the original line from the template.

FIGURE 1.4.53. Now we will glue the carbon fiber rods into the neck. We will use epoxy for this step. First, we cover the neck surface that will be glued to the fingerboard with masking tape, and using an X-ACTO knife, we cut out the slots for the rods. Since this is a very sloppy job, we use the tape to keep the neck surface clean.

FIGURE 1.4.54. Here are the rods glued into place. We have put a few strips of masking tape down onto the bench to mix the epoxy. This tape will easily pull up after the glue is set up, and cleanup is easy.

FIGURE 1.4.55. Here is the neck with both carbon fiber rods glued in place. Uneven areas will be sanded down after the glue is completely hardened. The next step is to take the truss rod and glue a thin wood veneer to the top of it. We use a medium viscosity superglue for this step. If you remember, we cut the truss rod slot 1/32" deeper than the thickness of the truss rod. This veneer will bring the surface of the top of the rod up to the neck surface. If the veneer is slightly below the level of the neck surface, glue a second vener over the first to fill this gap. If the veneer is slightly above the surface, it must be sanded with a belt sander to be the same level as the rest of the neck.

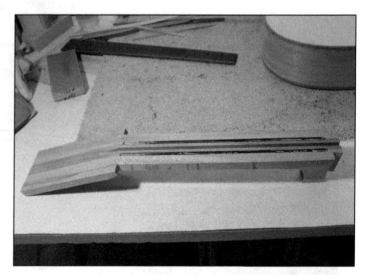

INITIAL NECK ALIGNMENT

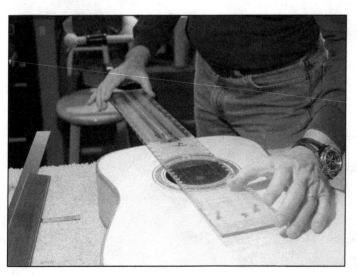

FIGURE 1.4.56. After the truss rod is in place, but before we glue on the fingerboard, we will put the neck into the dovetail slot and check alignment. The jig shown has a centerline on it, which we can use to check the neck to the centerline of the soundboard.

FIGURE 1.4.57. Once side-to-side alignment is checked, we need to check vertical neck alignment. For this, we place the fingerboard onto the neck (it's not glued yet) and place a sample bridge in its proper position on the soundboard. By placing a straightedge along the fingerboard, we can see how it lines up with the top of the fingerboard. We want it to just kiss the top of the bridge—up to about 1/32" higher. If it is lower or higher than this, we need to adjust the neck angle. It is easiest to do this now, before we glue the fingerboard on.

FIGURE 1.4.58. In our case, the side-to-side alignment was right on the money, but the neck angle was very slightly high. So to bring the angle down, we are pulling a strip of sandpaper along the thin shelves we created on each side of the dovetail, where the neck will rest on the sides of the guitar. To bring the angle down, we put the sandpaper between the neck and the side (with the sandpaper side up against the neck), push the neck down against the side, and pull the sandpaper up, toward the top of the guitar. To keep the side-to-side alignment true, we will do the same number of pulls on each side, checking our alignment every twenty or so pulls.

FIGURE 1.4.59. Here is the fit before we glue on the fingerboard. There will be some final fitting to do later, but this is pretty good for now.

GLUING THE FINGERBOARD AND HEADSTOCK LAMINATE

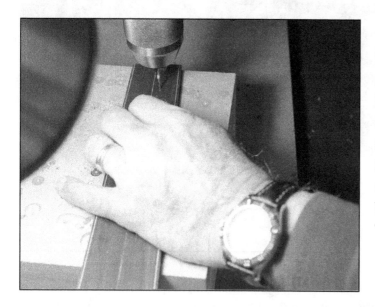

FIGURE 1.4.60. We are now ready to glue the fingerboard to the neck. First, we draw a centerline on the fingerboard and mark where we will drill two holes. The holes are drilled 1/4" away from the centerline, directly in the fret slots of the first and thirteenth fret for the steel string and the archtop. In the case of the classical, the holes will be drilled at the first fret and the eleventh fret. The holes are 1/16" in diameter.

FIGURE 1.4.61. Now, we center the fingerboard onto the neck exactly where we want it and drill holes directly into the holes we drilled into the fingerboard. The tape on the drill bit is marked at the 1/2" line, so the holes will go completely through the fingerboard and 1/4" into the neck wood.

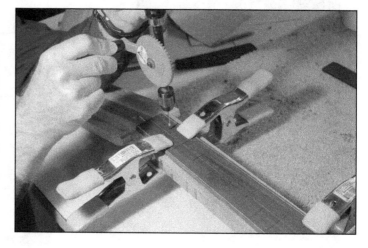

FIGURE 1.4.62. Now we will put a strip of 1/2" tape down the center of the underside of the fingerboard and apply Gorilla Glue to the portion of the board that will meet the neck. We are using a sample credit card blank for this purpose. We use Gorilla Glue for this step because we have found over the years that Titebond or other standard wood glues can inject water into the neck during gluing and often puts a slight warp into the neck. The Gorilla Glue has not caused this problem. We know several luthiers who use epoxy for this step, and there is no problem with epoxy. We just find it to be very messy, so the Gorilla Glue has been a good choice for us.

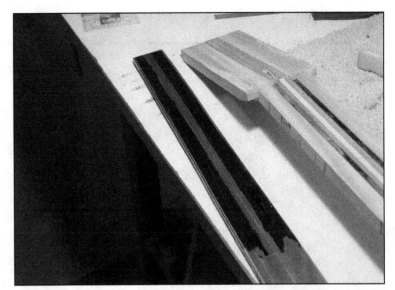

FIGURE 1.4.63. Once the glue is applied, the tape is pulled up, and we're ready to glue the board.

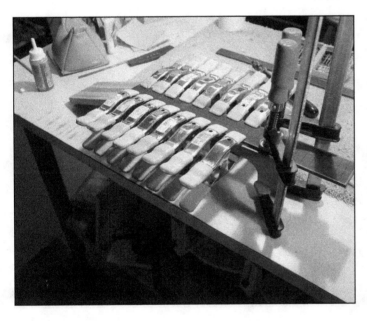

FIGURE 1.4.64. Once the fingerboard is put down against the neck, brads are put into the holes to ensure proper alignment. Next, we put several spring clamps on the fingerboard and two screw-down clamps to hold the fingerboard against the neck heel. The Gorilla Glue will expand to glue the wood over the truss rod to the fingerboard, but if we had left the center section of the fingerboard fully glued, the Gorilla Glue could seep down and impact the action of the truss rod. Using this technique, we have not had this problem. Right after gluing, we remove one clamp at a time and clean the glue squeeze-out.

FIGURE 1.4.65. Here is the glued fingerboard.

FIGURE 1.4.66. Now we will prepare and glue on the headstock laminate. For this guitar, the laminate will be a sandwich of a maple veneer (approximately .020) and a much thicker slab of Indian rosewood approximately .100 thick. The combined thickness is very close to 1/8". We have already glued the two pieces together and let them sit in clamps overnight. If they are unclamped and used too quickly after gluing, an uneven sandwich like this will curl, so we give it a lot of time. Even now, we want to work quickly, or the laminate could curl. We want to glue it to the headstock as soon as we can.

FIGURE 1.4.67. We now must prepare a rough nut for the guitar, so we take a piece of bone material 1/4" thick, 13/32" tall, and 2 1/4" wide. We are putting one edge of the nut on a jig that has the same angle as the headstock angle (15 degrees), and we will sand that angle onto the bottom of the nut.

FIGURE 1.4.68. Now we put the same angle onto one edge of the headstock laminate (if it's not obvious, this is the edge that will go up against the nut).

FIGURE 1.4.69. Remember that the fingerboard was glued to the neck with the nut edge exactly on the angled edge of the headstock. We have to measure from the back edge of the nut to the end of the truss rod, since we have to cut a gap in the headstock laminate to go over the truss rod.

FIGURE 1.4.70. With the truss rod measurements transferred to the headstock laminate, we make a rough cut on the band saw. We cut well inside the lines on this step because we want to file to the lines to make them look good.

FIGURE 1.4.71. We file the band-sawn edges and check the headstock laminate frequently on the headstock to make sure we don't file too far.

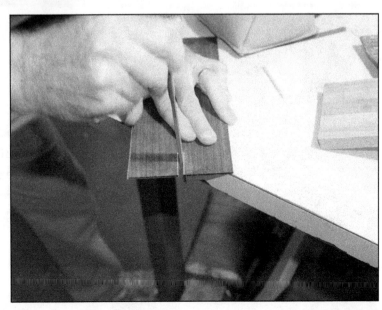

FIGURE 1.4.72. Here's a good shot of how it will all fit together. The front edge of the nut fits flush against the fingerboard, the bottom of the nut is flush against the face of the headstock, and the back of the nut will fit flush against the angled edge of the headstock laminate.

FIGURE 1.4.73. We now take our headstock template and trace its outline.

FIGURE 1.4.74. Now we clamp down the headstock laminate and drill a couple of holes on the outer corners of the headstock ears outside the area of the drawn headstock. You could also drill through the location of the tuning machines. The holes are 1/8".

FIGURE 1.4.75. We have placed 1/8″ dowels into the alignment holes. This helps ensure that we can get the headstock in the same position when we glue it down.

FIGURE 1.4.76. After we drill the holes, the alignment dowels are removed so glue can be applied to the surface of the headstock. Then the headstock laminate is placed back down where it belongs, and the dowels are put back in their holes. Once inserted, they are cut with a flush-trim saw.

FIGURE 1.4.77. We use a 3/4″ thick caul of MDF to evenly apply clamping pressure as we glue on the headstock laminate. We like to put the caul at the edge of the headstock laminate so any glue that squeezes out can be cleaned from the nut area.

SHAPING THE HEADSTOCK AND THE NECK

FIGURE 1.4.78. After the glue has dried, we screw down the headstock template through locations that the tuning machines will use later.

FIGURE 1.4.79. Next, we will cut around the template as closely as possible. It's always important to leave a comfortable margin so we don't cut up our template. Note that we have put some green masking tape on the hyoid portion of the headstock template. Since the template and the fingerboard are the same size, we want the headstock to be cut slightly larger so we can file it to size.

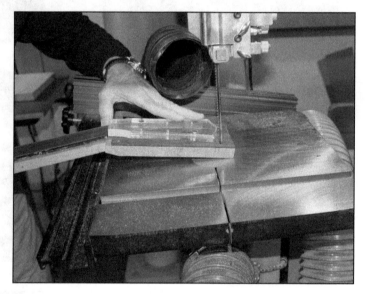

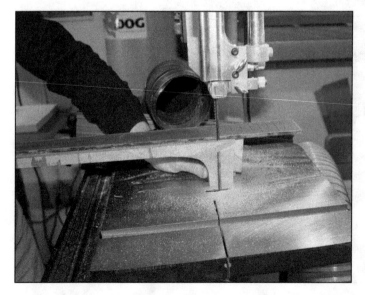

FIGURE 1.4.80. We also cut the edges outside the fingerboard as closely as possible. Again, we want to leave a good margin because cutting the fingerboard or its binding would be a disaster at this point.

FIGURE 1.4.81. We then use the headstock template as the routing template and rout the headstock using a flush-trim bit. You must be certain to push against the direction of the router bit—especially along the very top of the headstock—or it could kick back and possibly ruin the headstock, or cause an injury

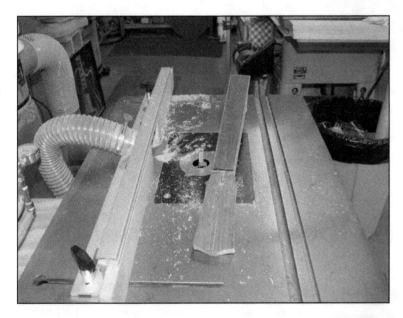

FIGURE 1.4.82. After trimming the headstock, we remove the headstock template and lower the height of the cutter so it will ride on the edge of the fingerboard. We will then use the fingerboard edge as a template to trim the rest of the neck to the fingerboard shape.

FIGURE 1.4.83. Now we will clamp the neck into a vise and chisel the edge of the truss rod slot to match the angle of the truss rod.

FIGURE 1.4.84. To mark the position of the tuning machines, we draw a line perpendicular to the centerline at the locations of the two screw holes used for the template. Then we find the center between these lines and draw a third line parallel to the first two. This gives the tuning machines 1 5/8″ spacing. Also, the machines are spaced in from the edges by 1/2″.

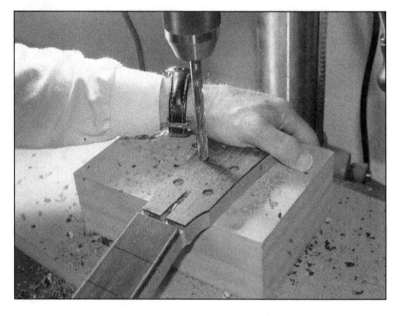

FIGURE 1.4.85. Time to drill the holes for the tuning machines. We will use a brad point bit 25/64 diameter (1/64″ larger than 3/8″). The reason for this size choice will become evident in the next photo.

FIGURE 1.4.86. We are going to use a 5/8″ counterbore with a 3/8″ pilot bit to bore out a 5/8″ diameter area around each tuning machine hole. Once the finish is applied, screwing the machines down while the finish is not completely cured causes ripples in the finish on the top of the headstock. The counterbore makes a break in the finish and prevents this problem. The reason we predrill a 25/64 hole is that a 3/8″ pilot bit will not fit into a 3/8″ hole, so we have to drill a slightly larger hole to use the 3/8″ pilot bit. The hole is still perfectly good for the tuning machines we will be using.

FIGURE 1.4.87. Here is the counterbore bit in use. The large collar is used as a depth stop for the bit. Note that it makes a slight burn mark around the hole. This is no problem, since we will be doing a lot of sanding on the surface of the headstock as we inlay our logo. It is important to clean the wood out of the counterbore bit after each drilled hole. Otherwise, excess wood builds up, and the drilled holes are not clean.

THE HEADSTOCK INLAY

FIGURE 1.4.88. Now we are ready to start on the inlay of our logo. We will start with two identical copies of the logo.

FIGURE 1.4.89. We will cut out one of the copies and glue it to the headstock. We will worry about the tail of the bird later and concentrate on the body and wings first.

FIGURE 1.4.90. We are now cutting out the body of the bird and will glue the individual pieces to a scrap of mother-of-pearl (MOP).

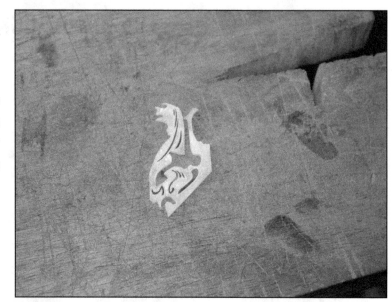

FIGURE 1.4.91. Here are all the paper pieces making up the body of the bird after they are glued to the scrap piece of MOP. We were lucky to be able to fit the bird's entire body onto the one MOP piece.

FIGURE 1.4.92. Now we cut out each of the pieces. We are staying slightly outside the lines, and we will file any uneven sections.

FIGURE 1.4.93. We use a small vise to hold each tiny piece of MOP as we file.

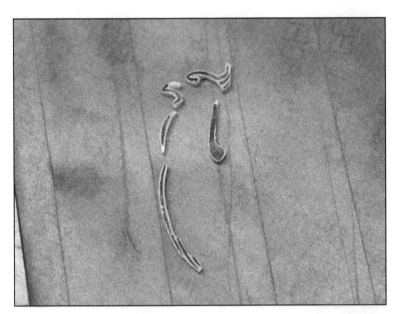

FIGURE 1.4.94. Here are all the pieces of the bird's body, cut out and filed. We have placed them on a board with masking tape, sticky side up, to keep the MOP pieces in place.

FIGURE 1.4.95. Now, we will focus on the wings. One set (on the left) will be done with green select abalam, while the other set will be done with pink select. This will give a slightly different look to each set of wings.

FIGURE 1.4.96. After cutting and filing, this is what the whole Phoenix bird, minus the tail, looks like.

FIGURE 1.4.97. Now we use a Dremel tool and rout out all the patterns glued onto the headstock.

FIGURE 1.4.98. Before we complete the placement of the bird's tail, we must get the truss rod cover made. We are using a piece of scrap from the headstock laminate, so the match will be a good one.

FIGURE 1.4.99. After shaping the truss rod cover, we sand the same angle onto the nut edge as we did on the headstock laminate.

FIGURE 1.4.100. Once we have placed the truss rod cover, we can determine the best placement of the bird's tail. The entire logo is shown in the photo. It was cut out with the Dremel and is ready to inlay.

FIGURE 1.4.101. Before we inlay, we use a brown Sharpie (to match the Indian rosewood), and smear ink inside all the routed holes. This will stain the superglue that we will use to glue the Abalam and MOP, and it will match the headstock.

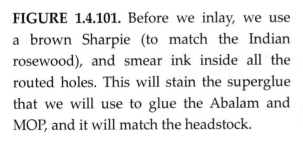

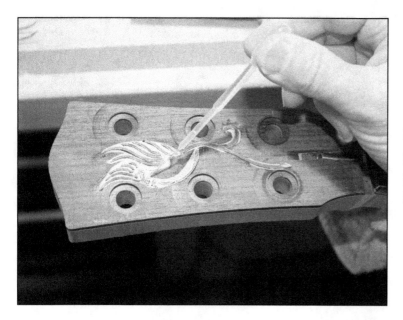

FIGURE 1.4.102. Now we put each cut piece into its respective slot and use a small pipette of superglue (thin) to secure the inlay in place.

FIGURE 1.4.103. After sanding the inlay flush to the headstock surface, you will typically find some gaps that weren't filled with glue. These gaps (some large and some very small) will often be filled with white powder from the inlay dust after sanding. Clean the gaps with an X-ACTO knife, blow the area clean with compressed air, reapply the brown Sharpie ink, and put more superglue into each gap.

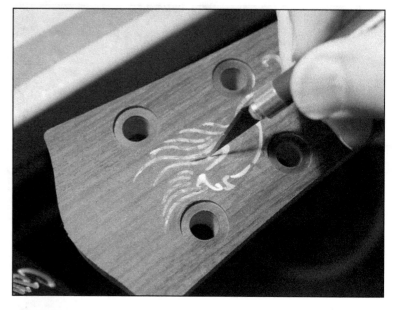

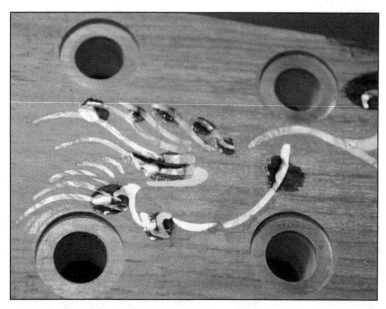

FIGURE 1.4.104. Here is a good close-up of the inlay after staining the gaps and regluing.

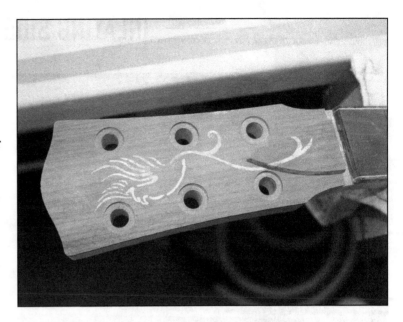

FIGURE 1.4.105. This is the final inlay after a little more sanding.

SANDING THE HEADSTOCK TO THE PROPER THICKNESS

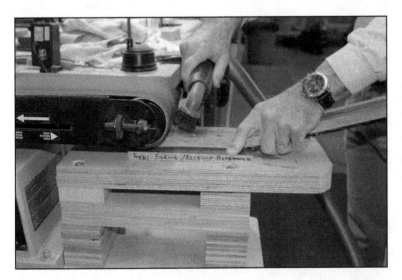

FIGURE 1.4.106. Here is the jig we use to thickness the headstock of our steel string and archtop guitars. The classical guitar uses the same basic jig but with a different size spacer to make its headstock the proper thickness.

FIGURE 1.4.107. Here is the headstock, sanded to thickness.

INLAYING SIDE DOTS

FIGURE 1.4.108. Now it is time to put in the side dots. We will use MOP side dots (2 mm). So we mark the position of the fret slots, mark the location for the dots (halfway between the frets), and drill a hole for each dot.

FIGURE 1.4.109. With all the holes drilled and the side dots properly placed in the holes, we use a drop of superglue to affix the dots. For this fingerboard, we can use superglue since the binding is a dark wood (Indian rosewood). If it were a light wood, like maple, the superglue could stain the maple a yellow color. In that case, we would use a drop of Titebond in each hole before we put in the dots. Remember, the dots should stick out slightly from the level of the binding.

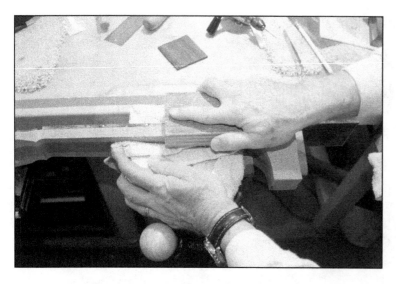

FIGURE 1.4.110. Last, we use a flat sanding board to sand the dots so they are level.

THE HEELCAP

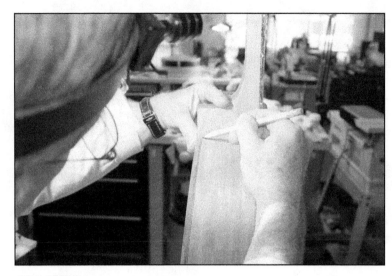

FIGURE 1.4.111. Now we will cut the heel. We cut our heel at the point that's level with the top stripe of the side purfling. In this case, we are going to put purfling under the heel cap to match the position of the side purfling. In this photo, we are marking the location where we will make the cut. We will make this mark on both sides of the heel.

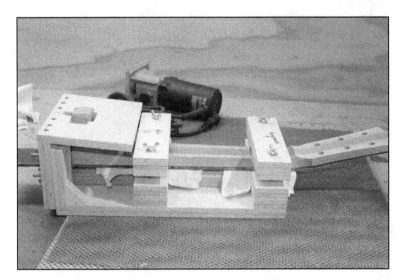

FIGURE 1.4.112. Here is the jig we use to cut the heel. This was copied from the website of Michael Bashkin. This jig is a great idea and makes the level of the cut and the angle very repeatable. I want to thank Michael for his permission to show the jig here.

FIGURE 1.4.113. We are going to cut the heel off exactly at the level of the top of the plane of the jig. In this photo, we are checking with a chisel that the jig level lines up with the pencil mark we made above in Figure 1.4.111.

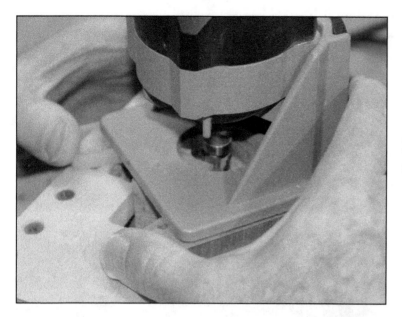

FIGURE 1.4.114. Here is a photo of the router cutting down the heel.

FIGURE 1.4.115. Here is the final heel cut.

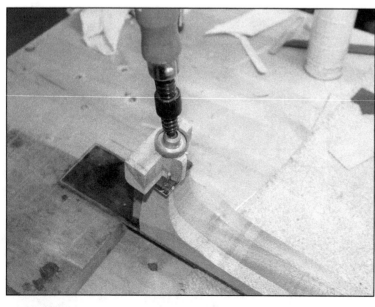

FIGURE 1.4.116. Now, we make a three-layer stack of black fiber, maple, and black fiber, with each being .020 thick. We then take a piece of Indian rosewood as a heel cap, glue the sandwich together, and clamp it to the heel. It makes it easier to drill small pilot holes in the corners of the heel to put in brads to keep the cap assembly from sliding during gluing and clamping. We will later pull out the brads and carve away the holes as we carve down the heel.

FIGURE 1.4.117. We leave the edge of the heel cap adjacent to the guitar side slightly overlapping since it would be a disaster for it to have a gap and making it perfect is difficult. This way, it only takes a few pulls of sandpaper to make everything level.

CARVING THE NECK

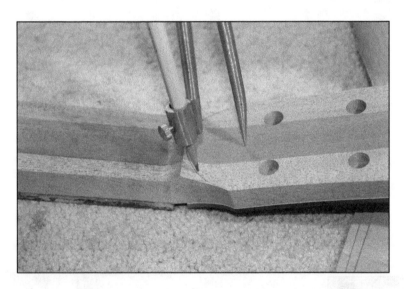

FIGURE 1.4.118. Since we are about to start carving the neck, we use a compass to mark where we will carve the volute.

FIGURE 1.4.119. We start carving by taking away some of the excess using the belt sander.

FIGURE 1.4.120. Next, we carve with a microplane. This tool works well because it does more cutting than grinding.

FIGURE 1.4.121. After doing some of the carving, we move up the neck and use a file to start shaping the volute.

FIGURE 1.4.122. We like to use a flat sanding board with 80-grit sandpaper attached to it to be sure the entire board is level all the way across.

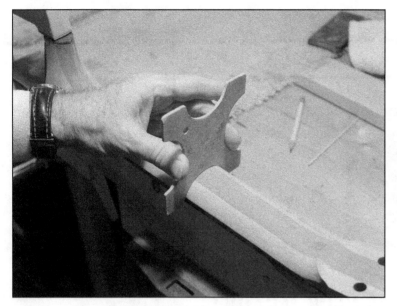

FIGURE 1.4.123. As the neck is being carved, we will use the template shown to check the radius of the neck as it slowly increases from the nut to the heel. The template is simply a square of fiberboard with a different arc cut on each side: 1″, 1 1/16″, 1 1/8″, and 1 3/16″.

FIGURE 1.4.124. In addition to checking the radius of the neck, we check the neck thickness using a caliper. Typically, at the nut (or just in front of the nut), the thickness is 13/16″ and increases by about 1/16″ to 7/8″ as you move down the neck to about the ninth fret. Some guitars increase in thickness by more than 1/16, but our customers tend to like this smaller increase.

DRAWING 1.4.2 Steel String Neck Profile
(at the nut)

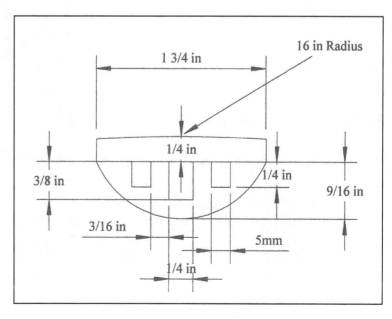

FIGURE 1.4.125. After all the rough sanding and filing has been completed, all the rough marks are sanded out with 220-grit sandpaper.

FITTING THE NECK (AGAIN)

FIGURE 1.4.126. After the neck carving is complete, we will recheck the neck alignment with a template that shows the neck center-line. We use the center seam of the guitar top to check this. In this case, we see that the neck is very slightly pointing off to the left by about 1/16" at the bridge. Now we will adjust the neck alignment.

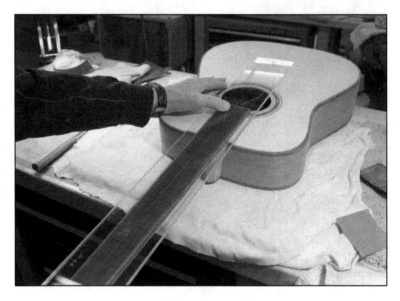

FIGURE 1.4.127. If the neck is pointing to the left, the sandpaper must be pulled straight to the left side to realign the neck. Once we get the alignment correct, we'll check the vertical angle. We don't want to adjust two angles at once. In this case, it took about fifty pulls of the sandpaper to get the alignment right.

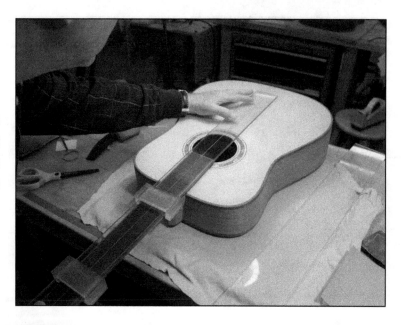

FIGURE 1.4.128. Now, we'll recheck the side-to-side alignment using a different alignment tool that is a little more accurate than the template. Now, the alignment is right on.

FIGURE 1.4.129. After making an initial check of the vertical alignment, we see that it looks very good, but once the side-to-side alignment is changed, the dovetail fit is slightly loose. We are going to shim the dovetail and refit it to be sure that it is tight and that the neck is perfectly aligned. When we're done, there will be almost nothing left of the shims. We'll almost completely carve them away as we make the final fit. In this photo, we're gluing on the new shims (small pieces of veneer).

FIGURE 1.4.130. Once the shims are glued to the dovetail, we are marking the head-block side of the dovetail with chalk.

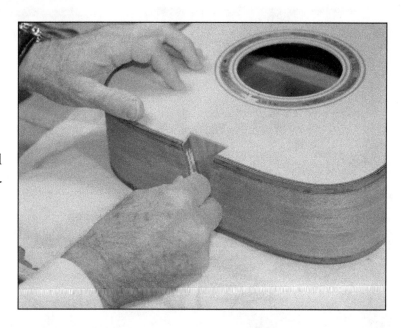

FIGURE 1.4.131. We put the neck into the dovetail to check the fit.

FIGURE 1.4.132. Here is the first fit of the neck after the shims are glued on. It is sitting too high, and we need to start shaving down the shims to make it fit.

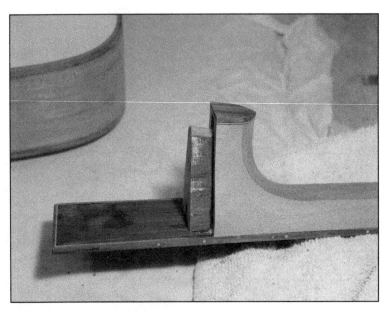

FIGURE 1.4.133. Once we pull the neck out of the dovetail, we can see the marks the chalk has left. This shows where our neck dovetail is hitting the body dovetail. We must make the dovetails hit as evenly as possible along their entire length so it is as strong as it can be. In our shop, we have seen many guitars with dovetails where the neck and body didn't have a good fit, and the gaps were filled with glue. This is not a good way to make a dovetail fit. The wood edges must meet very well and must be very tight.

FIGURE 1.4.134. We will start carving the shims back, especially where the chalk marks are located, to make the dovetail fit.

FIGURE 1.4.135. You can also use a file to trim the shims—but be careful not to scratch the heel cap. You can see that we have covered it with tape to keep prevent damage.

FIGURE 1.4.136. In this photo, the neck is perfectly fit into the dovetail joint. The neck overhang is touching the guitar top, and you can see that our heel cap purfling is lining up nicely with the purfling around the body.

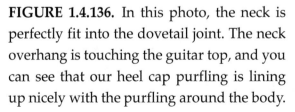

FIGURE 1.4.137. We do one final neck alignment check, both side-to-side and vertical. In this photo, we are measuring the vertical neck alignment using a test bridge and a straightedge. The neck aligns to a point about 1/32″ above the bridge—just about perfect.

Now, it is time to sand the body to prepare for finishing and time to make the bridge.

1.5
THE STEEL STRING BRIDGE

There are several ways to make a perfectly good bridge for a steel string guitar. Many builders have a template they use to draw the bridge profile onto a piece of ebony or rosewood, and then they cut close to the line and sand the rest of the way to get the shape of the bridge. Using a belt sander, they sand down the wings and shape the rest of the bridge. While this method can work well, it can have a couple of problems. First, each bridge will be slightly different. If one of the bridges cracks over time and needs replacement, a new bridge will have to be made. The bridge edges and pinholes may not line up properly with the old edges and pinholes, so the repair becomes sloppy and more difficult to do. We are going to show a method we learned from Charles Fox in a class on small-shop production. We want to thank Charles for his time, suggestions, and willingness to share his ideas with us (and his permission to put this information into this book). The following method for making a steel string bridge will help make the bridge dimensions very repeatable, very accurate, and with the jigs, much faster to make than doing each one separately by hand.

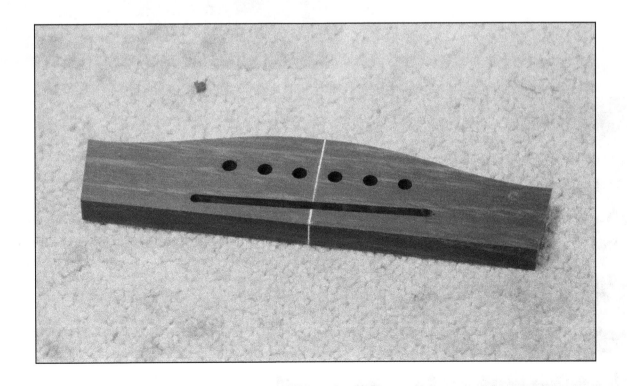

FIGURE 1.5.1. Starting with three very rough-cut bridge blanks, we will make two right-handed bridges (one for the steel string being made for this book) and one left-handed bridge.

FIGURE 1.5.2. First, we will sand one side flat and put one of the long sides through the jointer. This leaves us with two smooth sides at 90 degrees from each other.

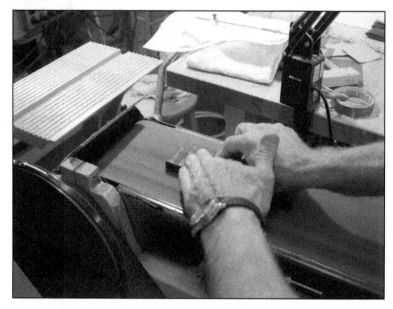

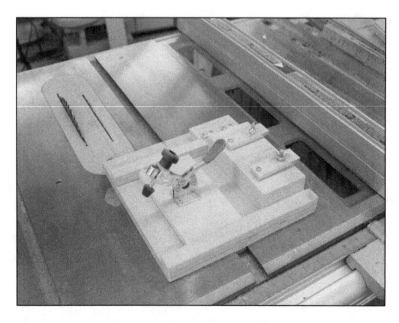

FIGURE 1.5.3. This is the first jig, which we will use to perform four steps that result in a perfect bridge blank with exact dimensions.

FIGURE 1.5.4. First, we lift the small, hinged flap at the upper right of the jig and make a small cut. Note the other end of the bridge must be overlapping the hinged line. The blank is still too long at this point.

FIGURE 1.5.5. Next, we flip down the hinge, place the freshly cut end against it, and cut the other end. With that, we have a blank that is the proper length. We don't have to measure it, since we had measured when the jig was made. Our bridge blank is 6″ long.

FIGURE 1.5.6. Next, we put the blank into its slot under the toggle clamp with the previously jointed edge against the jig and the rough edge up, and make another cut. This establishes the exact width of the bridge blank.

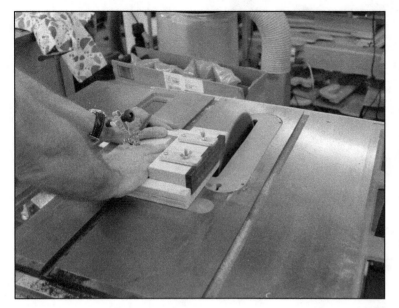

FIGURE 1.5.7. Last, we put the blank with the smooth side against the jig, reverse the side of the saw that we will use, and make the final cut for the blank thickness. We made the small clamps we are using by cutting and drilling pieces of 1/4″ thick, 1″ wide aluminum stock. A couple of small springs around the screws hold the clamps up when not in use.

FIGURE 1.5.8. Here it is, a nearly perfect bridge blank. Length, width, and thickness were completed within a few minutes, and all the blanks are the same. This will also be true of the next batch we make, and we don't have to set up equipment every time we do a batch of bridges.

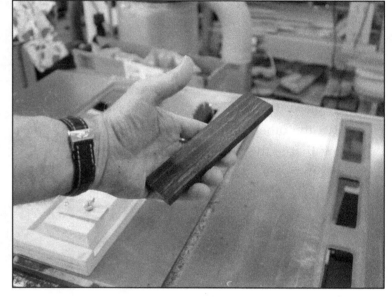

FIGURE 1.5.9. This jig allows us to drill two holes that eventually define each end of the saddle slot. Shown are two 1/8″ drill guides with the outside point of each hole being exactly 3″ apart and with the proper taper for the bridge. The goal is for the front edge of the saddle at the first string to be 1/8″ closer to the front of the bridge than it is at the sixth string.

FIGURE 1.5.10. This is the other side of the jig. The bridge blank fits tightly into the jig and is clamped into place with the wingnut screw.

FIGURE 1.5.11. We clamp a backer board to the bridge so as the bit comes through we don't get any chipping out of the wood. Then we drill the holes.

FIGURE 1.5.12. Here is the bridge with the holes drilled.

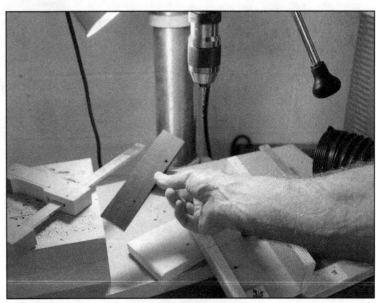

FIGURE 1.5.13. This is the next jig. It uses two small brass pins (each 1/8″ in diameter) sticking up about 1/16″ above the base level of the jig. Note that the line between the pins and the lines defining the router base guides are all parallel.

FIGURE 1.5.14. We now place the bridge blank into the jig, being sure that the brass pins seat properly into the holes we just drilled. The figure shows the proper positioning for the right-handed bridge. Note that the bridge blank can be put in upside down to create the proper positioning for the left-handed bridge.

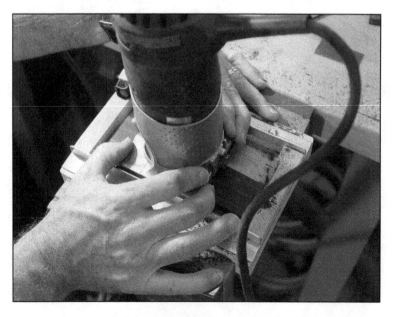

FIGURE 1.5.15. As you can see, the aluminum angle pieces are used to guide the laminate trimmer. The trimmer fits snugly in between the aluminum guides and rests on the bridge blank. The wood blocks on each end of the bridge blank mark exactly the travel that the laminate trimmer will take. Starting on the left side with the trimmer held against the wood block, the 1/8″ bit is in the hole drilled. As the trimmer is pushed along the aluminum guides, it ends in the other hole, as shown on the left.

FIGURE 1.5.16. Here is the bridge blank with the slot. Note that the brass pins in the jig must not stick up very high, because the router bit is sticking down into the hole. You must leave some distance between them so you don't ruin either the brass pin or the bit. The depth of cut in this case is 3/16″, and the total thickness of the bridge blank is 3/8″. A little will be taken off this dimension as we radius the bottom of the bridge and shape the top. The final thickness should be a little over 5/16″.

FIGURE 1.5.17. The next jig is used to shape the ends of our bridge. We have a taper on our bridge ends.

FIGURE 1.5.18. Here is the blank end being cut. The corner of the bridge blank is put directly on the edge of the jig, just where the cut is made. To make the cut on the other end, rotate the blank 180 degrees and flip it over. If you forget to flip it, you will end up having two parallel cuts for the bridge ends—probably not what you want.

FIGURE 1.5.19. Here is the blank after both ends are trimmed.

FIGURE 1.5.20. This jig will shape the back profile onto the bridge blank. Note that on the left side of the jig there is an angle that the bridge blank will fit into. It's also important to note that only half of the back profile will be cut at a time.

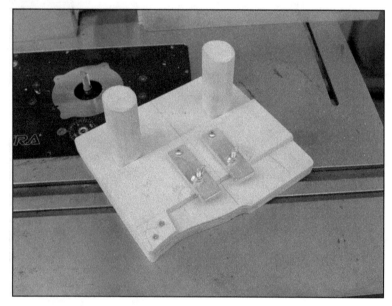

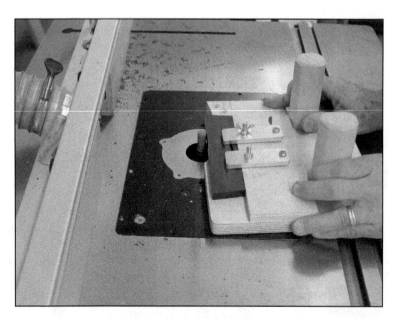

FIGURE 1.5.21. Here is the bridge in the jig with routing being done on one side. Don't try to cut the entire side down in one pass. It's better to make small cuts.

FIGURE 1.5.22. Here is the first half done.

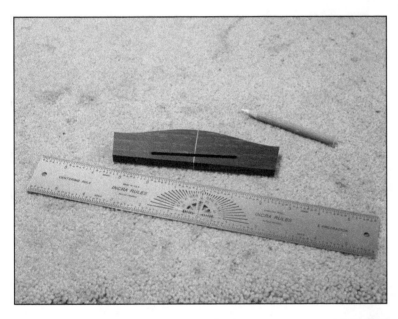

FIGURE 1.5.23. After rotating the bridge 180 degrees and flipping it, (it should be obvious how it has to be placed in the jig), we cut the other side. The result is shown. In addition, we use a centering scale to draw a centerline along the front edge and the top of the bridge.

FIGURE 1.5.24. This is a great jig we bought from LMI. Frank Ford designed it. It allows you to drill your bridge pinholes very accurately at several different pin spacings. We put this jig into a fixture that allows us to place our bridge against a block, center it against the centerline, and drill our holes (2 1/4″ spacing). This is how we make most of our bridges.

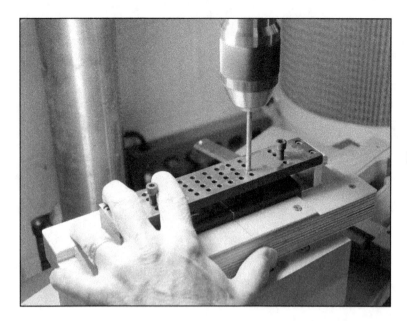

FIGURE 1.5.25. Now, we drill the holes.

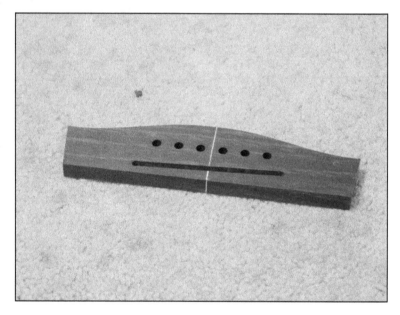

FIGURE 1.5.26. Here is the bridge with all holes drilled.

FIGURE 1.5.27. In order to cut the "wings" of the bridge, we use a small 4" belt sander purchased just for this step. We have put a platform on the base of the sander, which we use as a feeding table, and have screwed a couple of thin (1/8") guides for the bridge. Now, we push the bridge into the belt sander to create the wing.

FIGURE 1.5.28. Here is the view of this sander under the sanding belt. You can see the platform and the guides, which also include tabs that will stop the bridge from being pushed in too far. We owe many thanks to my friend Frank Finocchio for this idea on sanding the bridge wings.

FIGURE 1.5.29. The first wing, out of the sander.

FIGURE 1.5.30. Here are the three bridges we started to make—two right-handed and one lefty—all virtually identical in dimensions. The final step for these bridges is to sand a 25′ radius on the bottom of the bridges (since the guitar top will have a 25′ radius), and soften the harsh edges created by the router and sander and do a little shaping of the bridge top.

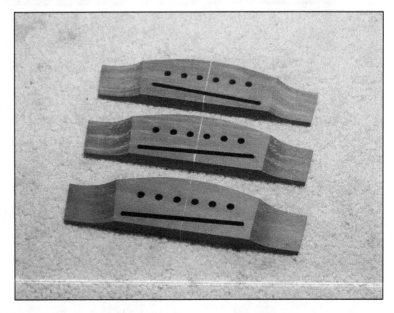

FIGURE 1.5.31. We will use this handle with a bone saddle blank that fits snugly into the bridge saddle slot.

FIGURE 1.5.32. Here is the bridge, held in place with the handle above, getting a 25′ radius sanded onto its underside. The 25′ radius jig is simply a mahogany board about 2′ long, with a 25′ radius sanded onto one edge, covered with sticky back sandpaper. This step will reduce the thickness of the bridge by about 1/32″. At this point the bridge is done, with the exception of some final shaping and rounding of the sharp edges that we will cover in chapter 1.7.

1.6
FINISHING
THE STEEL STRING GUITAR

Putting a high-gloss, high-quality finish on a guitar is not easy. You should not assume that you will get it right on the first try, so you should practice finishing on either a piece of scrap or on a cheap solid-body guitar to master the basics before you try it on an acoustic guitar that you have spent many hours getting to the point of finishing.

We are going to start this chapter by doing a thorough job of sanding. It is easy to get most of the surfaces clean on the guitar, but the areas around the joints are places that glue spots can remain. If you don't get the glue spots clean, they are likely to show up under the finish and are much more difficult to sand out once the finish is being applied. It is important to understand that for the case of the steel string guitar, we will finish the body and the neck separately.

SANDING AND SURFACE PREP

FIGURE 1.6.1. We start by using a random orbital sander to go over all surfaces, using 220-grit sandpaper. If your guitar has a cutaway, you won't be able to use the sander in the cutaway, so you will have to do that section by hand. Also, practice using the random orbital sander on scrap before you try it on your acoustic. It is easy to tilt the sander and create a divot in a critical surface that you cannot hide, so be sure you understand how to use the sander. You will be able to save time and create a smooth surface ready for finish.

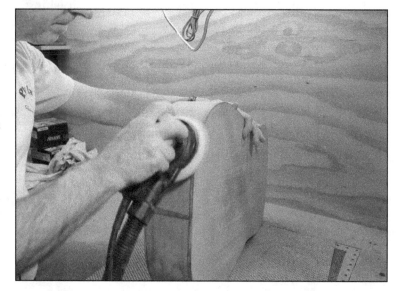

FIGURE 1.6.2. Here, we are using the random orbital sander on the side of the guitar.

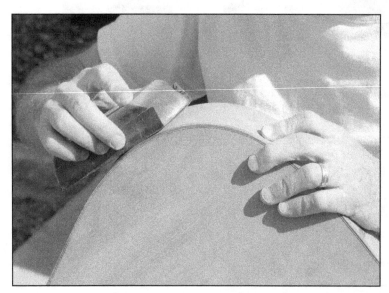

FIGURE 1.6.3. We will often go outside, where the light is much better, to do the final sanding. We can see glue spots in sunlight much easier than we can under the light in the shop.

FILLING THE GRAIN

FIGURE 1.6.4. Once the sanding is done, we tape off the edge of the top. We are going to fill the grain of the sides and back with epoxy, and we don't want anything getting on the top. There are many good ways to fill the grain, but this has worked out very well for us. I want to thank John Greven for walking us through this process. It was very helpful.

FIGURE 1.6.5. We now use a vacuum clamp from LMI to hold the body, using the same vacuum pump that we have shown before.

FIGURE 1.6.6. The epoxy we are using is System Three Silver Tip Epoxy from Jamestown Distributors.

FIGURE 1.6.7. Now, we mix the two parts of the epoxy, using pipettes to put the epoxy into the mixing cup. We are using a very accurate jeweler's scale, so we measure our amounts by weight. After the epoxy is mixed, we put in about 3 to 4 percent of Cab-O-Sil by weight. Cab-O-Sil is a thickening agent, and though it is white, it doesn't add any white color into the grain. With the small amount of epoxy we're mixing, only a little over a teaspoon of the Cab-O-Sil is necessary.

FIGURE 1.6.8. Initially, the mix is very lumpy, but after a minute or so of stirring, it has smoothed out and looks like this.

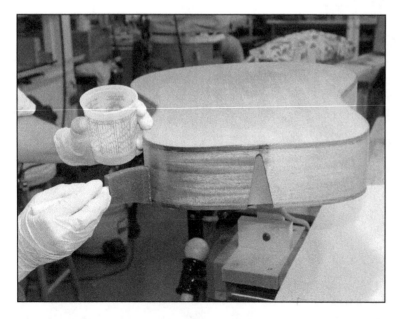

FIGURE 1.6.9. Using a foam brush, we apply the epoxy to the guitar body, sides first.

FIGURE 1.6.10. Next, we apply the epoxy to the back. After applying, you should use a credit card blank or squeegee to smooth the surface the best you can. Very thick or lumpy surfaces will be difficult to sand down later.

FIGURE 1.6.11. Once the epoxy is applied and smoothed out, we put the body into our spray booth, where we can turn on some lamps and heat the air by a few degrees to help the epoxy dry faster. The hardener we are using is a fast-cure hardener, but it still takes several hours before it can be sanded. Therefore, if we apply the first coat early in the day, we can get a second coat done before the end of the day. In most cases, at least two coats are needed. This mahogany has a lot of deep grains, so it will probably take three coats.

FIGURE 1.6.12. Next, we spread epoxy on the neck. First, we spread it on the front, back, and sides of the headstock, then on the heel and the fingerboard overhang.

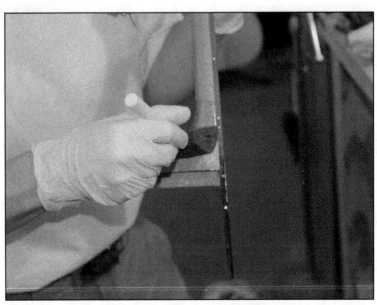

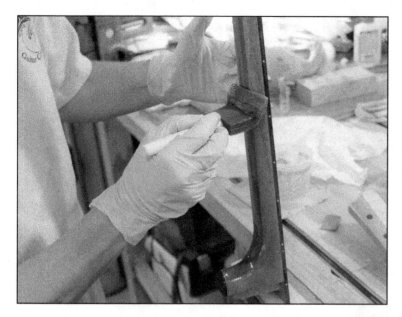

FIGURE 1.6.13. Now, we clamp the finger-board overhang into a bench vise and apply epoxy to the rest of the neck.

FIGURE 1.6.14. We will use a glove (like the ones being used in the photo) to help spread the epoxy down the neck to be sure the application is smooth. Be sure that you don't push against the neck, putting stress on the finger-board overhang in the vise. Note that pressure is being applied on the back of the neck with the glove and on the front of the neck (with the fingers of both hands). The fingerboard is taped off for the epoxy step (and through finishing) to keep it clean.

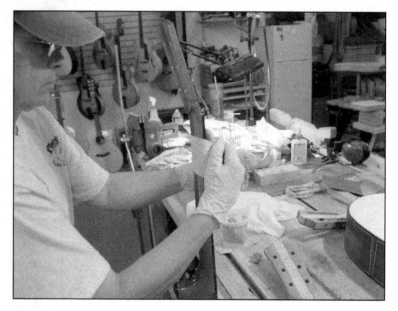

FIGURE 1.6.15. Here is a photo of the sand-paper we use for sanding out the epoxy. Also, as you can see from the view of the steel string back, the grain looks perfectly normal with the epoxy. Now, it's time to level the epoxy layer. We will use either 400- or 600-grit paper, depending on the thickness of the epoxy application.

FIGURE 1.6.16. We use the same sander as before, and the Abranet shown above attaches to the sander with hook-and-loop.

FIGURE 1.6.17. As you can see here, we have encountered a glue spot. It shows up as a light discoloration, this time on the Indian rosewood on the end graft. We will have to scrape down to the wood and sand the glue spot down. There is really nothing lost here, since we have to put on at least one more coat of epoxy. However, it is a good idea to carefully look at the entire surface and check for any more spots.

FIGURE 1.6.18. Here is a small oval scraper being used to scrape away the epoxy down to the glue spot. Once we have this and any other glue spots taken care of, we can reapply the epoxy. We will also sand the neck, but due to its curved surfaces, we have to sand by hand instead of using the random orbital sander.

FIGURE 1.6.19. After reapplying epoxy, we sand again. The goal is to fill the grain but leave a very thin layer of epoxy. This will typically take two to three applications of the epoxy to get the results we need. If you jump too quickly to finish before the grain is truly filled, you will have to spray more coats, and since lacquer will sink over time, the grain will likely become visible.

FIGURE 1.6.20. To sand the flat surfaces of the neck and headstock, we use a small, hard rubber sanding pad available at local auto paint stores.

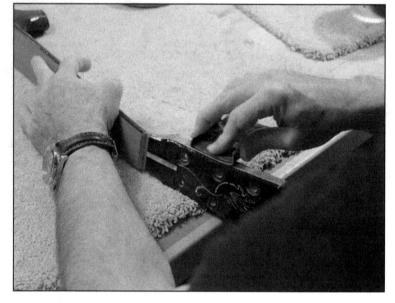

FIGURE 1.6.21. For the long, curved portion of the back of the neck, hand sanding is the best. At this point, which is probably the final sanding before spraying, we are using 600-grit wet/dry sandpaper. It is very easy to sand through, in which case, another coat would have to be applied.

FIGURE 1.6.22. Once we're happy with the grain fill, we will use a pipette filled with naphtha to help loosen the tape we put on the guitar top to protect it from the epoxy.

PLACEMENT AND TAPING OF THE NECK AND BRIDGE AREAS

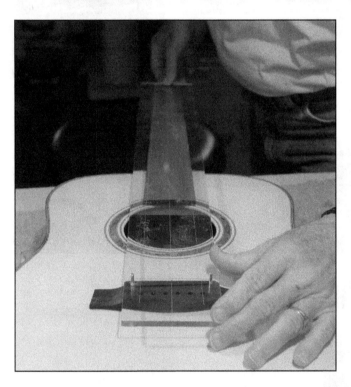

FIGURE 1.6.23. Now it is time to place the bridge. We made a plexiglass template with brass posts that fit exactly into the holes at each end of the bridge. We have one template for every scale length we use. It is an easy template to make, and we know the bridge will be in the correct position. The template has a centerline as well as scribed lines that represent where the outside strings will be. Once the bridge position is located, we will use a pencil and trace a very faint line around the bridge.

FIGURE 1.6.24. We want to make a piece of masking tape that is about 1/8″ smaller all the way around than the bridge. We put tape on the underside of our bridge, and using an X-ACTO knife, we cut about 1/8″ inside the edge. We peel off the excess and the under-sized piece of tape.

FIGURE 1.6.25. It is very difficult to see the pencil line that outlines the bridge location, but the tape is put right in the center (or as close as we can get—exactness is not critical here). Now, be sure to erase the pencil line, using a very soft eraser.

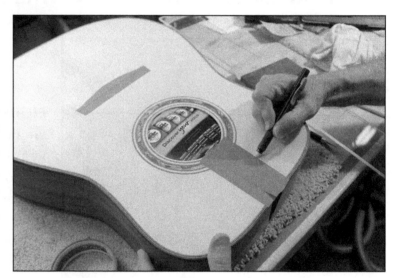

FIGURE 1.6.26. Next, we put the neck back on, trace around the fingerboard onto the body, and put tape about 1/16" inside that line. Note that the sound hole has been stuffed with paper, and a string box lid has been put over the paper. All residual pencil lines must be erased. We like to use a white eraser since it leaves less residue on the guitar top.

SPRAYING THE GUITAR

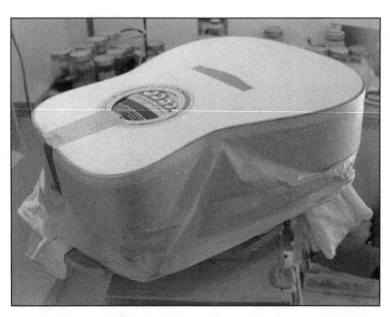

FIGURE 1.6.27. Now we tape off the sides of the guitar. This guitar will have a two-tone sunburst on the top, and we are going to do colors next.

The first color coat we will spray is a coat of amber shellac. It is sprayed over the entire top of the guitar, including the rosette and the purflings. It is not dark enough to require taping off the rosette and purflings. We always spray shellac on the top under our lacquer as a sealer, even when we are not doing colors. In this case, we are also using the shellac for color.

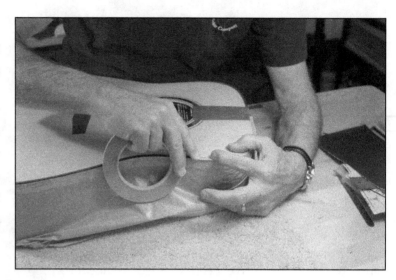

FIGURE 1.6.28. After spraying the first color (the amber shellac), we will tape off the purflings around the guitar edges with 1/4″ masking tape. The next color will be a cherry red sunburst, and we want the purflings to remain their natural color. The red color is mixed in with blond shellac. We always spray our colors mixed in with shellac. It sprays well and looks good under our water-base lacquer.

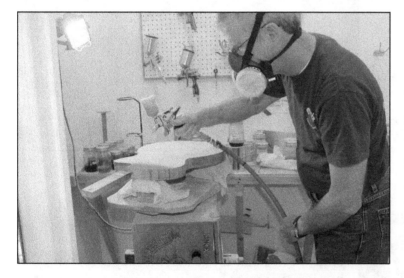

FIGURE 1.6.29. Before we actually spray the color on the guitar, we spray it on a test board. We want to check how the gun is spraying and make sure there is no spitting or dripping from the gun before we spray the guitar—any gun malfunction would be a disaster at this point. Since the body will be sitting on a lazy Susan so we can rotate it as we spray, we want to be sure it is also functioning smoothly.

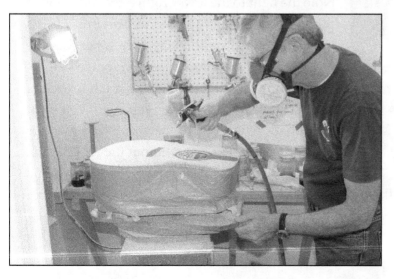

FIGURE 1.6.30. Next, we spray the sunburst along the edge of the guitar. We will typically have to spray at least two coats to be sure the color is dark enough and the band of color is wide enough. Also, it is imperative that you don't try to spray too dark a coat all at once. This could cause a drip to form, and this is a very difficult problem to fix, requiring sanding away all the color and starting over. Spray light and use multiple coats to get the best results.

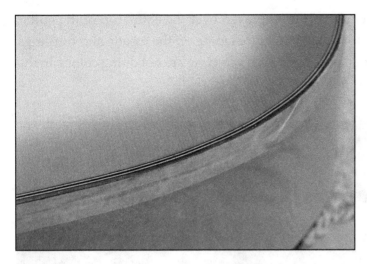

FIGURE 1.6.31. Here is a very common problem when you spray colors. Sometimes some of the color will bleed under the masking tape. Try to locate all the spots that have bled and use an X-ACTO knife to scrape away the color.

FIGURE 1.6.32. The color is being scraped off the purfling with an X-ACTO knife.

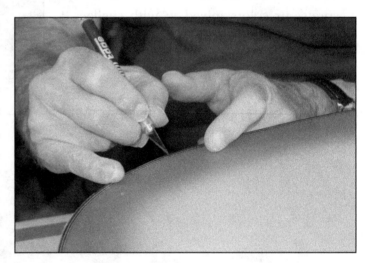

Once the purflings have been scraped as needed, you will have to use a paintbrush to touch up the areas where the amber shellac has been scraped away just to keep the bindings the right shade. Also, the tape and paper covering the sides of the guitar are removed, since we are about to spray clear coats. You will probably have some tape residue clinging to the sides of the guitar, so wipe off the residue with naphtha before spraying.

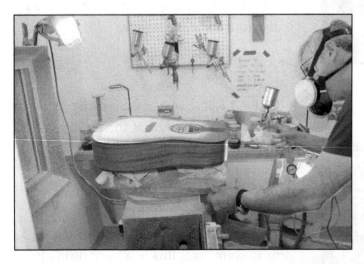

FIGURE 1.6.33. This is a pretty good angle showing our spray booth. Clear coats are being sprayed on the sides and top (first day of spraying). Note the light to the lower right—the reflection of this light can be seen as the sides are sprayed. The guitar is rotated on the lazy Susan, keeping the reflection in view as the sides are sprayed all the way around. The light at the upper left is used to see the reflection as the top is sprayed. You must keep these reflections in view as the spraying is done. If you try to spray without the reflection in view, you really can't see how good and even a job of spraying you are doing. On the far left is the exhaust, which is a filter in front of an explosion-proof fan. Even though we spray mostly water-based lacquer, the colors, mixed in shellac, are flammable because the shellac is mixed with alcohol.

FIGURE 1.6.34. The top of the guitar is being sprayed. Note the reflective light in the upper left being used to be sure the spray is even all the way across. Also note that the first two coats right after the color has been applied are light, dry coats. If you spray too heavily right away, the color can bleed into the upper layers and look very bad. The coats sprayed on the sides must be lighter than those sprayed on the top to avoid dripping. It's OK because we will spray twice as many coats on the sides as we will on the top or the back.

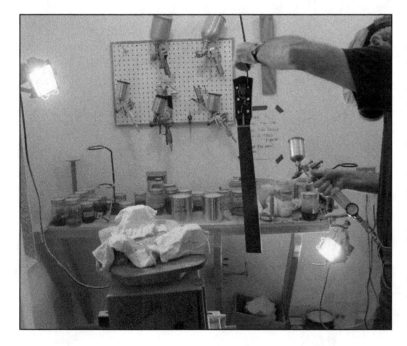

FIGURE 1.6.35. On the first day, we will spray five coats on the sides, top, and neck. Be sure to keep the spray reflecting in the light to make sure the spray is even. Also, you must spray the neck very lightly to be sure it doesn't drip.

The second day, we will spray five coats on the sides, back, and neck (as well as on the truss rod cover).

If we are spraying at a cooler time of the year (since our shop isn't heated), we will leave some hot lights on in the spray booth to bring the temperature up a couple of degrees and accelerate curing.

After the first spraying, we will lightly sand the surface flat using 400-grit sandpaper. This is a wet sanding. We will dip the sandpaper in water, and sand the surface. After sanding a few strokes, the excess water is wiped away. You want to sand the surface flat, but you have to use judgement, and not go too far. It's better to leave a few uneven spots than to sand through the finish.

SANDING AND BUFFING THE FINISH

FIGURE 1.6.36. After the first sanding, four or five additional coats are sprayed. Then, we wet-sand the surface by hand using 600- to 800-grit sandpaper, followed by 1200-grit paper. This sand-out is easier than the first, since the final coats went onto a very smooth surface. Using the spraying and sanding schedule we've presented results in the final finish thickness being between .005″ and .007″.

FIGURE 1.6.37. Once the sand-out is complete, we start the buffing process on the coarse buffing wheel. We use the coarse wheel both with and against the grain to get out as many scratches as possible.

FIGURE 1.6.38. During the buffing process, we will often put the guitar under a strong light to check the surface.

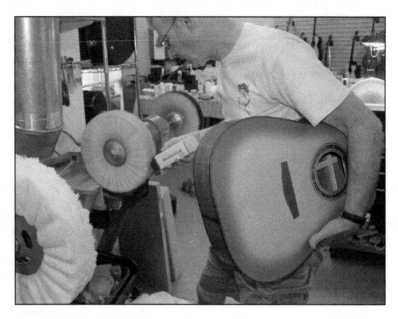

FIGURE 1.6.39. Be sure to put buffing compound onto the wheel every few minutes. This is yet another reason to practice finishing on a cheap piece of wood before you try on your nice acoustic. If you put too much buffing compound on the wheel, it will leave residue on the surface that is difficult to remove. If you use too little, the wheel will not be very effective.

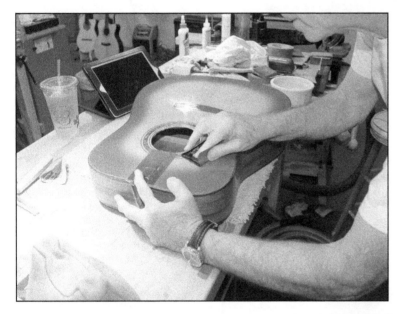

FIGURE 1.6.40. When you find a small bump or blemish, use a hard rubber pad and sand lightly with 2000-grit wet/dry paper (we use it wet in this case), then buff the area out. Note that if you sand too hard, you risk sanding a visible hollow into the surface (or sanding through).

FIGURE 1.6.41. After buffing with the coarse wheel, we then buff with the medium and fine wheels. Be sure that your final run on the buffer is with the grain.

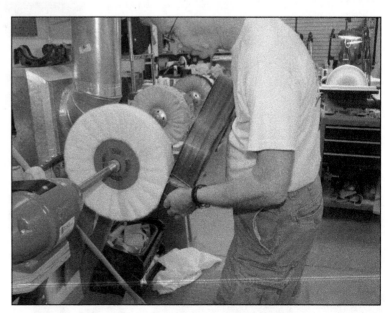

FIG, 1.6.42. Another important point in buffing is to be sure that the wheel starts on a flat part of the surface. It can go off the guitar on an edge, as shown in the figure, but it should *not* come onto the guitar on an edge, as shown in the next figure. On the sides, we will often buff against the grain as shown, but you cannot buff all the way across the side using this method. You must turn the guitar over and buff the other half of the side to continue against the grain. We will then buff with the grain to get a very thorough buffing before moving on to the medium and fine wheels.

FIGURE 1.6.43. Never let the buffer come onto your guitar on an edge, as shown in here. This can cause the buffer to grab the edge and throw the guitar to the floor, so always be very sure that you carefully bring the buffer onto the guitar on a flat surface.

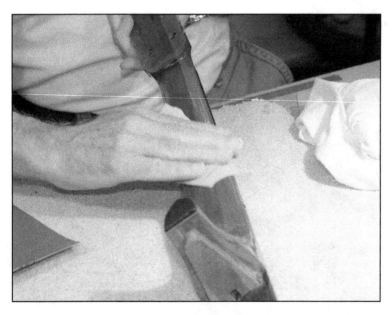

FIGURE 1.6.44. Once we're happy with the body, it's time to sand the neck. We will start with 600-grit sandpaper, then use 1000-grit sandpaper to sand the shaft of the neck. We will not buff the neck shaft unless requested to do so, because most of our customers like the feel of the neck with a satin finish instead of a gloss finish. However, we will sand the back and top of the headstock with 1200- to 2000-grit and buff them.

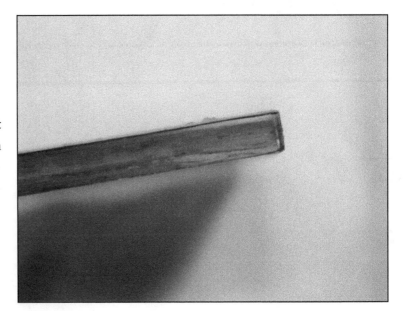

FIGURE 1.6.45. Notice the discoloration at the edge of the fingerboard. We have had a sand-through. This can be very common—especially on corners and edges.

FIGURE 1.6.46. We keep a jar of our finish on hand, just in case we get a sand-through.

FIGURE 1.6.47. Now, we apply the finish to the area of the sand-through. It could take several applications to get enough finish on the spot to be able to sand it flat. Once that is done, and the rest of the neck is sanded out, we will buff the headstock and the heel. We like to buff the heel, because it will be next to the guitar body, which has a high gloss, and we think the neck heel looks better with the same degree of gloss as the body.

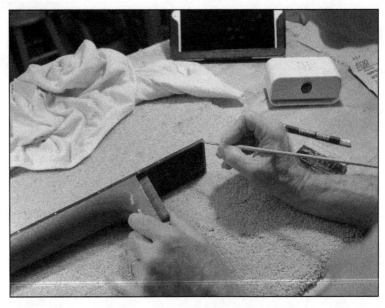

1.7
STEEL STRING FINAL ASSEMBLY

Once we're happy with the finish of the body and the neck, it is time to work on the final assembly of the guitar. If the neck was perfectly aligned prior to finishing, the alignment after finish should be very close. However, it needs to be checked.

GLUING THE NECK AND THE BRIDGE

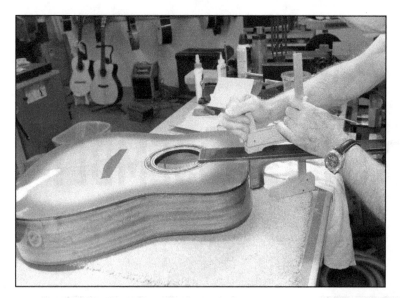

FIGURE 1.7.1. First, we must clamp the neck onto the body.

FIGURE 1.7.2. Next, we check the neck alignment with our neck template. This template allows us to check the centerline of the fingerboard with the center seam of the guitar top.

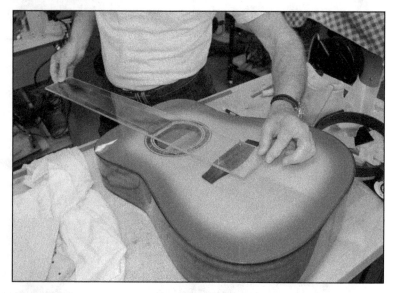

FIGURE 1.7.3. Even if the neck alignment is perfect, you will likely have to make a few pulls with sandpaper between the neck heel and the body, since there will be some finish residue on the heel at the neck joint. If the alignment is slightly off, more pulls will be required to get things back into proper alignment before moving on.

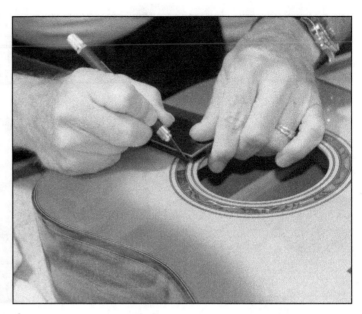

FIGURE 1.7.4. Once our alignment is correct and the neck is clamped down (not glued), we use an X-ACTO knife to scribe around the fingerboard, where it will be glued to the guitar top. Note: we like to use the back of the X-ACTO blade, because it gives us more control. Do not try to scribe with long strokes, since this is a good way to make a disastrous mistake. Make very short, controlled (1/4″ or so) strokes.

FIGURE 1.7.5. Here is a shot of the scribe line we just made. Now it is time to remove the material where we want the fingerboard to glue to the guitar top.

FIGURE 1.7.6. Using a very sharp chisel, we get under the edge of the lacquer and lift it to the scribe line. This step takes practice. You must be very careful not to go beyond the line and to not dig into the top. If the finish has had a chance to cure for a couple of weeks, this step is much easier, and the finish chips away. However, if you are in a hurry and the finish is not fully cured, it could be leathery and will peel. You have to be very careful if this is the case because if the finish is still soft, the guitar case will create dents and patterns in the surface of the finish. It is best to hang the guitar so it will not be resting against any surfaces until the finish has cured.

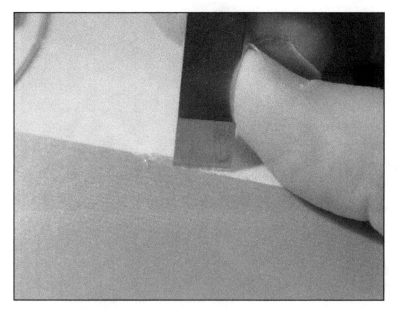

FIGURE 1.7.7. Once the material has been lifted with the chisel, the chisel can be turned vertically and used as a scraper, with the edge on the scribe line, to pull the material away from the line. This is assuming that the scribe line does not go completely through the lacquer. If the scribe line does go through the lacquer, the material will fall away once the chisel gets underneath and lifts it up. You must be very careful not to scribe too deeply. You don't want to go far into the top wood.

FIGURE 1.7.8. Now we're ready for gluing. The fingerboard overhang has glue already applied, and glue is being spread on the dovetails.

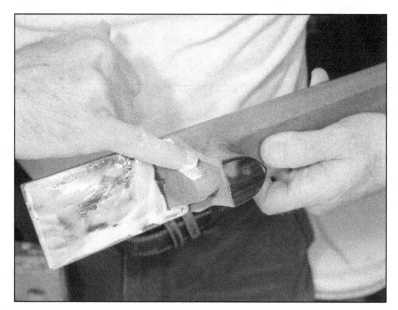

FIGURE 1.7.9. We apply two clamps at the edge of the guitar back to about the fourteenth fret slot. We want the clamping pressure to be as vertical as possible. You can see glue squeeze-out already starting to form under the clamps.

FIGURE 1.7.10. Next, we put a clamping caul in the sound hole under the fingerboard overhang. The caul is designed to go around the upper face brace and allow us to clamp directly onto the underside of the guitar top.

FIGURE 1.7.11. Here is the neck and fingerboard overhang, all clamped up. Time to clean up the squeeze-out.

FIGURE 1.7.12. We use a very soft, wet cloth and lightly wipe off the excess glue all the way around the fingerboard overhang.

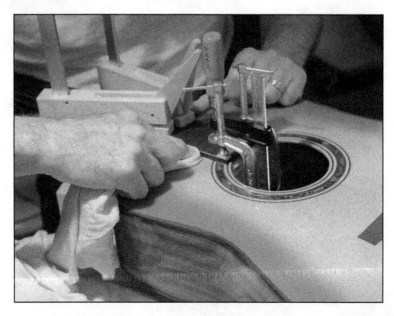

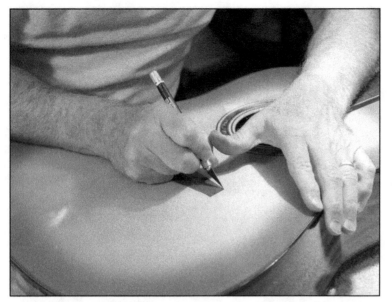

FIGURE 1.7.13. Once the neck and fingerboard have been clamped for about forty-five minutes, it's time to scribe for the bridge. Actually, Franklin—the maker of Titebond—says that you only need to leave the wood clamped for about twenty minutes. We tend to be conservative in this area. In this photo, we're scribing around the tape that marks the bridge location.

FIGURE 1.7.14. After you cut around the tape, lift a corner and start to peel the tape. You may need to cut more if you didn't cut all the way through the finish the first time. Remember to peel the tape toward the bare spot.

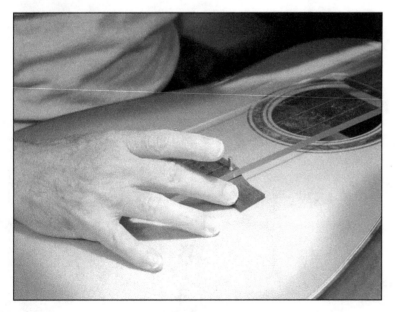

FIGURE 1.7.15. Now it is time to place the bridge using the alignment template.

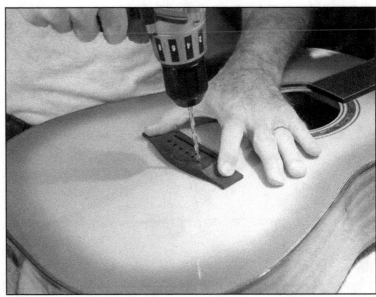

FIGURE 1.7.16. The next step is to remove the template while leaving the bridge in its correct location. Then, 3/16" holes through the two bridge pinholes on the ends.

FIGURE 1.7.17. Once the holes are drilled, we place two 3/16" brass pins into the holes to hold the bridge in place very tightly while we perform the next step: scribing around the bridge.

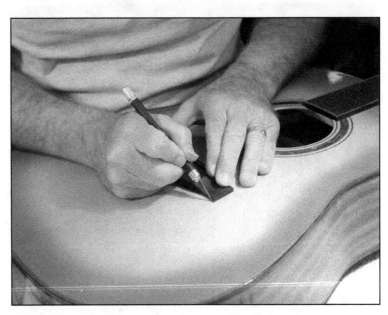

FIGURE 1.7.18. Now, while the pins are holding the bridge in place, we scribe around the bridge, exactly as we did with the fingerboard overhang.

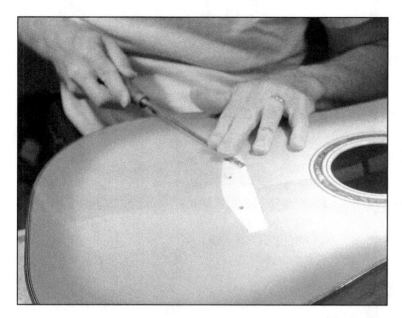

FIGURE 1.7.19. Next, we use a chisel to lift and scrape away the lacquer up to the scribe line. This is a step where a long-neck chisel works very well. It's easier to hold the chisel flat against the surface.

FIGURE 1.7.20. In the last view we had of the bridge, it still had sharp edges (just as it did when it came out of the final shaping jig as described in the chapter on the steel string bridge). Before we glue it down, we want to do some hand shaping and round the edges to soften the shape of the bridge. Here, we are using a belt sander to take off some of those sharp edges.

FIGURE 1.7.21. After sanding away as much material as possible on the belt sander, we will then use a coarse grit of sandpaper and shape the remainder by hand.

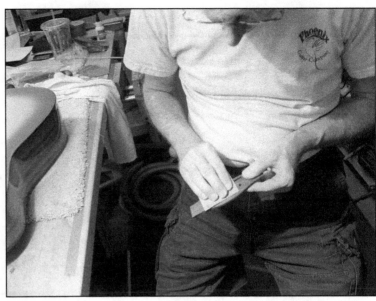

FIGURE 1.7.22. Once the desired shape is achieved, we will go up in sandpaper grits. Starting at 120, we go to 220, 320, 400, and 500 before buffing the bridge.

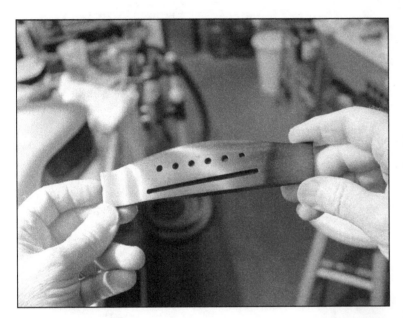

FIGURE 1.7.23. Here is the final bridge, sanded, buffed, and ready to glue.

FIGURE 1.7.24. Now, we glue the bridge. We like to put a thin coat of glue on both the guitar top and the bridge so we get a better glue surface with fewer gaps.

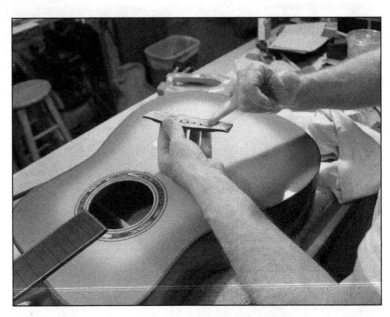

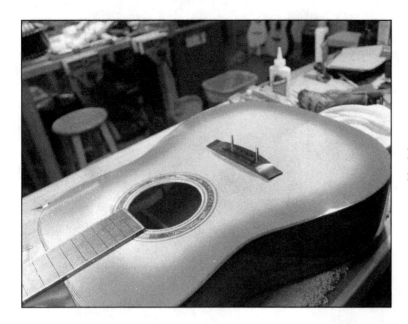

FIGURE 1.7.25. We again put the brass pins into the holes to align the bridge to the top.

FIGURE 1.7.26. Once the clamps are applied, you can see that we have pretty even glue squeeze-out.

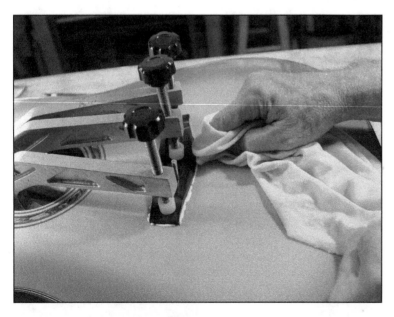

FIGURE 1.7.27. As before, we use a wet cloth to clean up the glue.

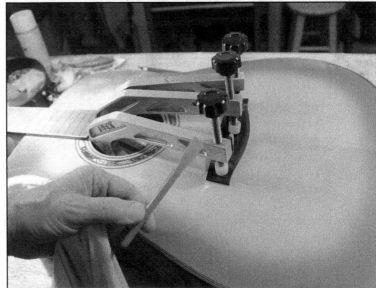

FIGURE 1.7.28. We often use a small plastic spatula as shown to help clean up glue squeeze-out.

FIGURE 1.7.29. We will wrap the plastic spatula in the wet cloth and use it to reach under the clamps and get the most difficult squeeze-out.

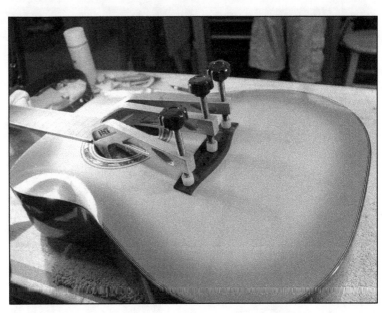

FIGURE 1.7.30. After a short while, we will pull out the brass pins, before the glue is dry and they are very difficult to remove.

FIGURE 1.7.31. We like to wait until the next day after gluing the neck to work on it. The next step is to check the neck for straightness and adjust the truss rod until it is straight (remember, it's a two-way rod, so we can adjust it either way as needed).

FIGURE 1.7.32. First, we chalk the fingerboard, and then we use a radiused fingerboard sander to get the fingerboard completely level from the nut to the twenty-first fret. We have always liked to level the board on the guitar. It helps eliminate the "hump" that is so common on many acoustic steel string guitars at the fourteenth fret.

FIGURE 1.7.33. After the fingerboard is level, we inlay the fret markers. In this case, we're putting in a basic pattern of MOP dots, which is what our customer ordered.

We like to get the fingerboard level before we inlay the markers because we don't know how much sanding might be required to level the board, and we don't want to risk sanding away a particularly shallow inlay.

FIGURE 1.7.34. We use a hand drill to drill the holes because we feel we have more control over the depth. Also, we use brad point bits for this operation to get the holes in the right spot.

FIGURE 1.7.35. Now we use a little thin super-glue to glue in the dots. Just running the super-glue around the edge of the dots is sufficient for the glue to seep around and under the dots. Next, we again level the board and the dots. We sand the board using 120- through 500-grit sandpaper and do a small amount of buffing to be sure there aren't deep scratches that we've missed.

THE FRET JOB

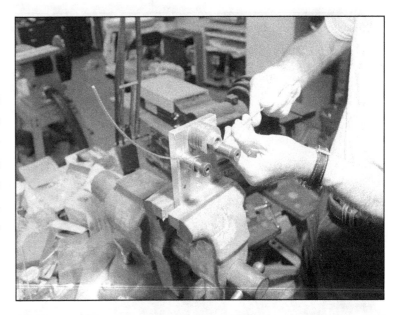

FIGURE 1.7.36. Now that the fingerboard is level, we bend our fretwire in our homemade bending machine. There is nothing very scientific about this job. We simply want the wire to be bent to a smaller radius than the fingerboard. Our fingerboard radius is 16", and our bender will bend the fretwire to about a 12" radius.

FIGURE 1.7.37. We now have to clean out the fret slots. First, we will get rid of any glue in the slots. We already know there is some glue in the first and thirteenth slots from when we used the pins for alignment when gluing the fingerboard to the neck. Shown is a Stew-Mac fret slotting tool—very handy for this job.

FIGURE 1.7.38. Now, we measure the depth of each fret slot all the way across. It's common for some debris to be at the edges of the slots. We want the slots to be at least 3/32" deep, and where it's not, we have to clean them out.

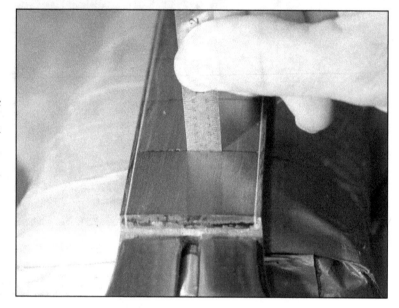

FIGURE 1.7.39. Here is another fret cleaning tool from Stew-Mac. This one does an excellent job of cleaning at the edges of the slots.

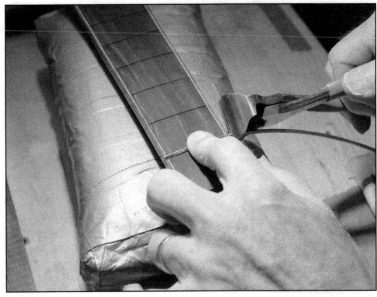

FIGURE 1.7.40. Now, we take our fretwire, lay it across the fist fret, and cut—with a little overlap on each side. We repeat this for each fret all the way up the fingerboard.

FIGURE 1.7.41. As each of the frets is cut, they are placed in a board as shown with numbered holes responding to each fret. This helps us keep each length of fretwire assigned to the proper fret.

FIGURE 1.7.42. After all the frets are cut, we take each fret, hold it up to its respective slot, and, using a Sharpie, mark slightly inside the purflings on both sides, by about 1/32".

FIGURE 1.7.43. Using the Sharpie marks to align the fret with the fret tang nipper (another very handy tool from Stew-Mac), we cut the fret tangs.

FIGURE 1.7.44. Here is the rough-cut fret. This is about right. The tang edges are about 1/32″ from each end of the fret slot. The fret will flatten slightly, pushing the edges of the tangs slightly outward as the frets are pounded into the slots. Therefore, we don't want the edges to be too close to the edges of the fret slots.

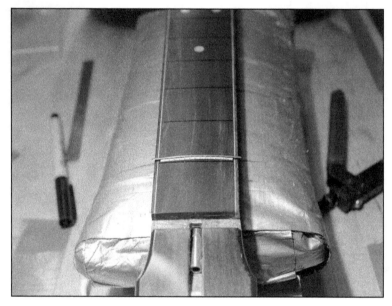

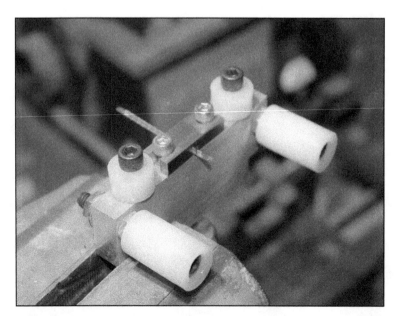

FIGURE 1.7.45. This LMI tool helps clean the fret tangs after they've been cut. The tang nipper usually leaves some residual material that needs to be filed away so the fret bead will sit flat on the binding,

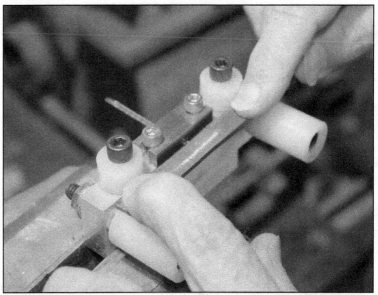

FIGURE 1.7.46. Here's the tool in action. Using a fine file, rolling it on the plastic rollers, and filing the fret tang residue flush with the underside of the fret bead.

FIGURE 1.7.47. Here we have squeezed some Titebond onto the fret slot using a glue syringe. We wiped the excess away with a damp rag. Now we're ready to start fretting. One additional note: We do not consider this to be "gluing" in the frets. The Titebond won't stick to the frets. We simply use it to fill all the gaps between the fret and the slot. It helps make the frets very tight in the slots. If you ever have to remove the frets, simply heat them with a soldering iron to melt the glue, and pull them out as you normally would.

FIGURE 1.7.48. Before pounding in the fret, you must be sure the fret is properly seated in the slot. The tang must be vertical, and the fret must be aligned properly side-to-side in the slot. At this point, firmly tap the fret into the slot. Be sure you don't tip the hammer, or you'll likely hit the fingerboard and make crescent-shaped dents that will need to be sanded.

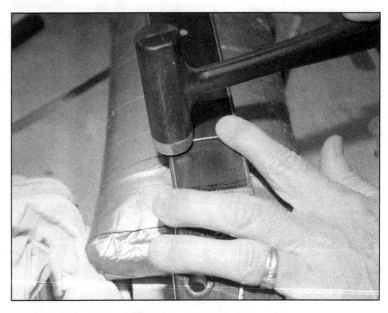

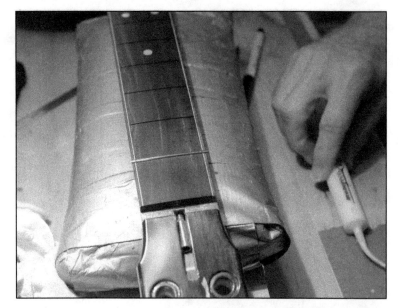

FIGURE 1.7.49. Here is the first fret in the slot. We will repeat this process through the sixteenth fret. Note the glue syringe on the right. We like to put a patch of masking tape on the corner of a bench so the glue does not drip onto the bench.

FIGURE 1.7.50. We use a Taylor fret buck to help pound in the final few frets over the guitar body. The fret buck helps disperse the hammer blows off the thin wood of the guitar top.

FIGURE 1.7.51. The fret buck holds the upper face brace very solidly so you easily can pound the final frets into the fingerboard without damaging the guitar top.

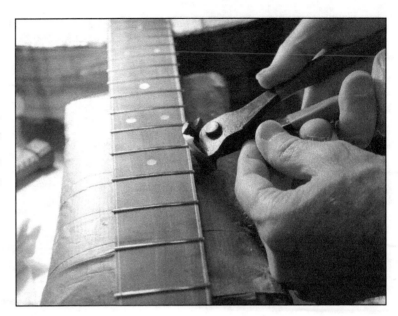

FIGURE 1.7.52. After all the frets are in, the next step is to use a fret nipper and cut off the fret ends. Don't push too hard on the fingerboard or the bindings or you'll leave marks that will be very difficult to sand out.

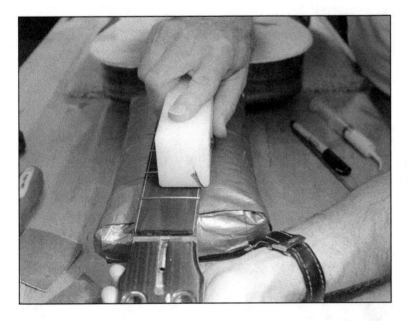

FIGURE 1.7.53. Once all the fret ends are nipped, we use a Stew-Mac fret-end file to file the fret ends to a 35-degree angle.

FIGURE 1.7.54. Here is what the fret ends should look like after filing. They must be even with the edge of the fingerboard (no overhang) and should all be a consistent angle.

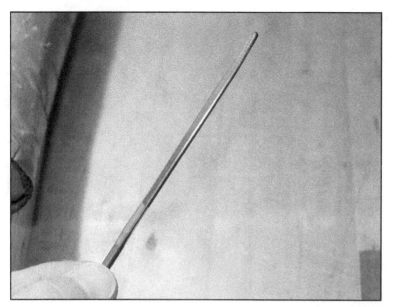

FIGURE 1.7.55. We will now use a three-corner fretting file that is smooth on the corners to file the fret corners. Though we have filed the fret ends, their edges are still sharp and must be filed and smoothed off to make the frets ready to play.

FIGURE 1.7.56. The file is used with a turning motion from the fingerboard up to the top of the fret and then from the other side. Note: You are not trying to grind away a lot of material here. You simply want to remove the burrs and sharp edges. After each stroke, feel the fret with your finger. Once it feels smooth, you are done.

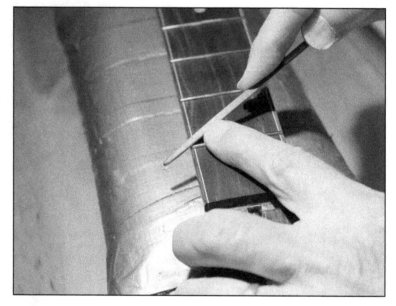

FIGURE 1.7.57. Here is a shot of the final fret end. Note that the edges have simply been softened. The basic shape of the fret end has not been changed.

FIGURE 1.7.58. Before we go on, we must make sure the fingerboard is straight. For this, we use another Stew-Mac tool that fits over the frets and shows whether the board is straight. We will adjust the truss rod until the neck is straight. After a fret job, the fret tangs are likely to force the neck into a slight back bow.

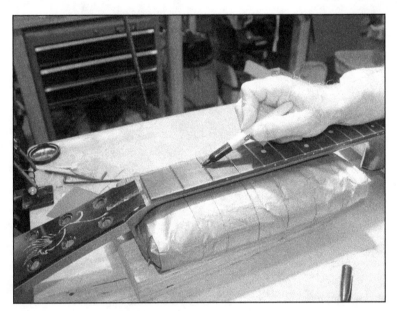

FIGURE 1.7.59. After the neck is straightened, a black marker is used to mark the tops of all the frets.

FIGURE 1.7.60. Next, we use the same curved sanding block that we used to sand the fingerboard to level the tops of the frets. We use 220-grit sandpaper for this step and sand very lightly. This step is called fret leveling.

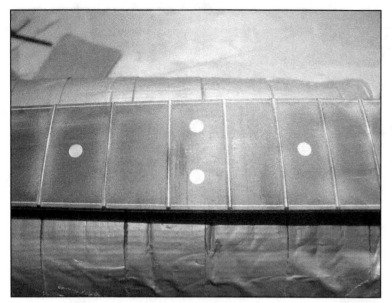

FIGURE 1.7.61. Not all the frets will have the same degree of sanding. Some will be sanded fairly flat and some will only be scratched, but once they all have been marked by the sanding block (all the way across), the tops are level, and you can move to the next step-fret crowning.

FIGURE 1.7.62. Here is the first fret being crowned with a diamond crowning file. It is critical that you check the fret many times with the light in different angles to verify that you have just barely filed up to and including the flat spot created by leveling. Don't file the fret too low in this step or you'll have to relevel it.

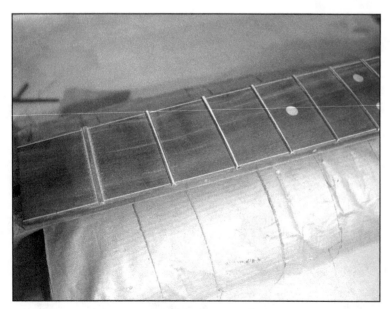

FIGURE 1.7.63. Here you can see the first fret, all crowned. The second fret is ready to be crowned.

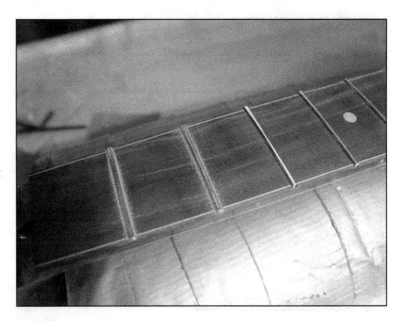

FIGURE 1.7.64. After a few strokes with the crowning file, you can see the shiny band across the center of the fret on the second fret (on the right). This is the remaining flat spot caused by leveling.

FIGURE 1.7.65. After a few more strokes with the crowning file, you can see that the shiny flat spot on the top of the second fret has gotten thinner. We're nearly done with this fret. After a few more strokes, it will look just like the fret on the left, and we will move on to the next fret. This process must be repeated for every fret.

FIGURE 1.7.66. Once all the frets have been crowned, they must be polished because they are still very rough. For this step, we tape off the fingerboard, leaving the frets accessible for sanding.

FIGURE 1.7.67. We now sand the frets with Micro-Mesh. We start with 1500 grit, then use 1800, 2400, and 3200. This will make the frets very shiny and ready for playing.

FIGURE 1.7.68. Leaving a protective over on the top of the guitar, we now buff the surface of the fingerboard, which also gives a little more polishing to the frets.

NUT, SADDLE, AND BRIDGE PREPARATION

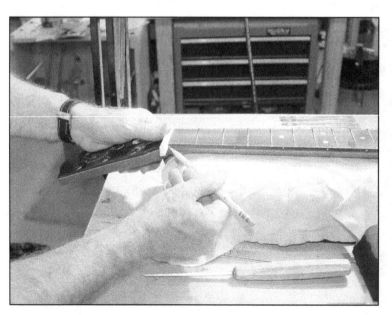

FIGURE 1.7.69. Now we take the nut that we briefly worked on earlier and be sure it still fits in the nut slot. The slot may need some cleaning if finish got into it. Once the nut can be fit into the slot, mark the ends, saw them close to the lines, and sand them to the lines with the disc sander. Use a fine file to get the edges as perfectly even with the nut slot as possible.

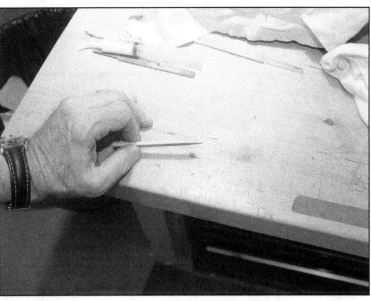

FIGURE 1.7.70. You need to make a half-pencil using a belt sander. The half-pencil must be at least long enough to reach from the nut to the second fret.

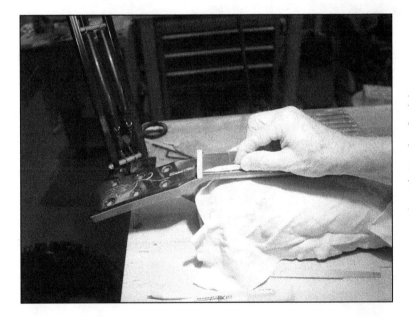

FIGURE 1.7.71. Now, draw a line on the front edge of the nut with the half-pencil resting on the first couple of frets. This will establish approximately how deep the string slots will be cut (but not exactly). It's an approximation only.

FIGURE 1.7.72. Using the disc sander, we sand the top of the nut to about 1/32" above the line drawn by the half-pencil.

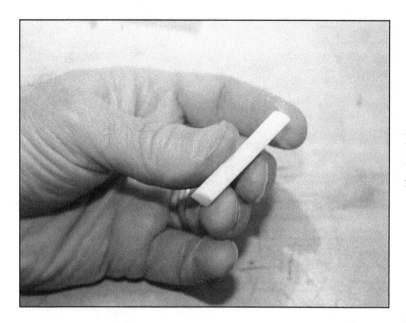

FIGURE 1.7.73. Using a sanding block and a fine file, we round off the back edge of the nut and file it smooth.

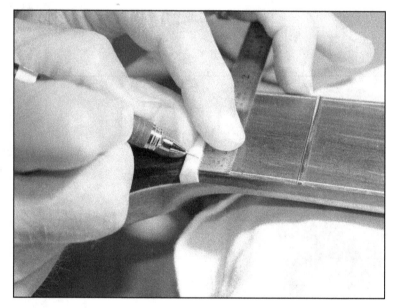

FIGURE 1.7.74. Next, we mark the two outside strings using a ruler that will mark thirty-seconds of an inch. We mark 1/8″ (4/32nds) for high E and 5/32nds for low E because the low E string is significantly fatter than the high E string, and this measurement makes the outer edges of the strings very nearly the same distance from the edge of the fingerboard. Use a very thin pencil for this step.

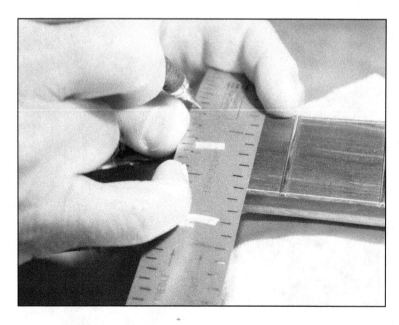

FIGURE 1.7.75. Now, using a Stew-Mac string spacing rule, we find the two outside string marks, and the rest of the string positions are automatically shown in their proper positions. We then draw the string position marks.

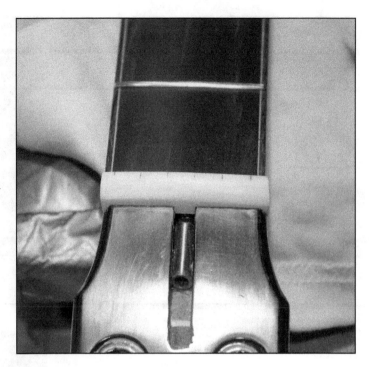

FIGURE 1.7.76. Here are the string position marks, shown on the nut.

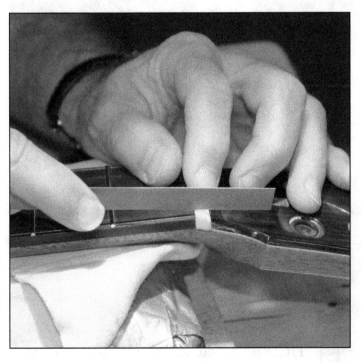

FIGURE 1.7.77. Now, we will use a set of nut files and file a very shallow slot directly on each of the position marks (we're not trying to get the final depth of the slot at this time). Be sure your slot goes directly on the mark. This may take a little practice, but it is critical that the string spacing is nice and even. We are putting light strings on this guitar, so the files we are using from high E to low E, are as follows:

.016 (for a .012 string)
.020 (for a .016 string)
.028 (for a .025 string)
.036 (for a .032 string)
.046 (for a .042 string)
.056 (for a .053 string)

You always want the slot to be rounded on the bottom and slightly wider than the string. If the slot is too tight on the string, you can get that irritating "click" as you try to tune a string and it catches on the nut. If the slot is too loose, the string may not sit in the right position in the slot.

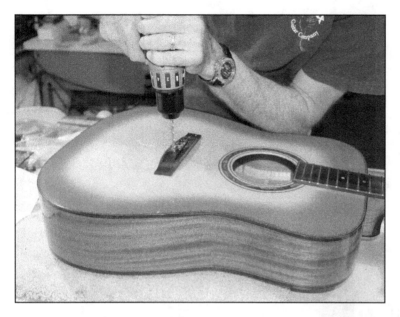

FIGURE 1.7.78. Now, we will prepare the bridge side. First, we finish drilling the bridge pin holes using a 3/16″ drill bit.

FIGURE 1.7.79. Next, chamfer the edges of the bridge pin holes. There are a couple of good ways to do this. First, you can use a hand countersink tool as shown.

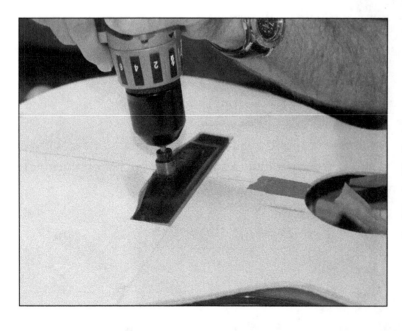

FIGURE 1.7.80. Another good way to chamfer the hole edges is using another Stew-Mac tool made for this purpose. It works well and gives very consistent results. Be sure to cover the guitar top when you're doing a job like this over it.

FIGURE 1.7.81. It's time to put in the bridge pins. However, they won't fit until we ream the proper taper into the existing holes.

FIGURE 1.7.82. We are using a 3-degree tapered reamer to properly shape the bridge pinholes. We will make a few turns, then check the bridge pin, then make a few more turns, then check, and so forth. We want the bridge pins to drop almost all the way down the hole and with only the lightest tap be all the way down. You don't want the pins to be too tight in the holes, because if you push a bridge pin down when it's already too tight, it can split the bridge. It's probably better for the pins to be slightly loose than slightly tight, but it's better to make them perfect.

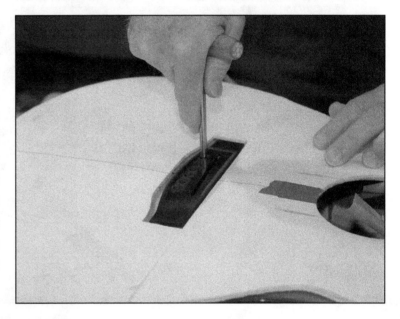

FIGURE 1.7.83. We will now use a tiny saw for cutting slots in the bridge pinholes to make room for the strings. Even though we are using slotted bridge pins, the slots are not wide enough for the A and low E strings to fit. Therefore, we saw a shallow slot in the pinhole to allow for the string to fit while the bridge pin can go completely down.

FIGURE 1.7.84. Now we put in the tuning machines. We need to use a reamer to fit the machines into the holes we originally drilled. Be careful here because it only takes a few gentle turns with the reamer to make the fit too loose. You want a slightly snug fit—but not a tight one. You can easily split the headstock if you push the tuning machines in too hard.

FIGURE 1.7.85. We will now fit the saddle. Upon first check, the saddle we have (1/8") is slightly too wide for the slot, so we are sanding it using a block.

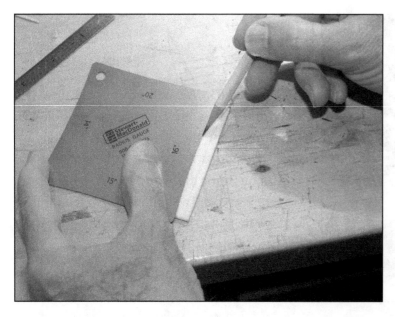

FIGURE 1.7.86. Once the saddle fits into its slot, we draw a 16" radius arc high on the saddle (higher than it will actually be—this comes from a little experience), then we sand the saddle down to the drawn arc line and put it into the saddle slot in the bridge. Note that we have not yet compensated the saddle or rounded the top of the saddle. That will come later.

THE STRINGS AND THE SETUP

FIGURE 1.7.87. Next, we put on the strings. This is the way we do it, shown on the D string. Bring the string over to the B string post to give the proper amount of slack and proper number of turns around the post, and put the string through the D hole. Then, bring the string end around the back of the string post (toward the center of the headstock) and put the string under itself, as shown in the next photo. By the way, for the A string, pull it over to the high E, and for the low E, pull the string over to the treble side of the nut. Reverse this set of positions to string up the treble strings.

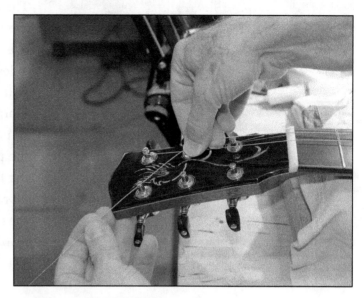

FIGURE 1.7.88. We put the string under itself and pull up on the string. We now start to tighten the tuning machine, and the string will tighten on itself, locking itself onto the tuning peg. The strings will not slip if you use this technique to string your guitar.

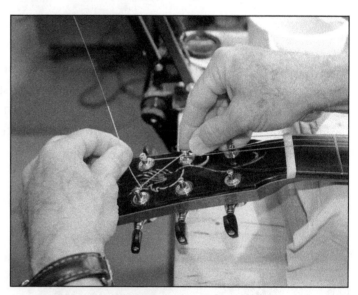

FIGURE 1.7.89. Once the string is tuned, the "tail" can be cut off.

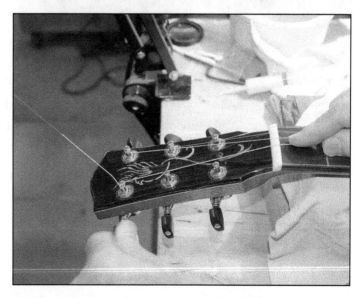

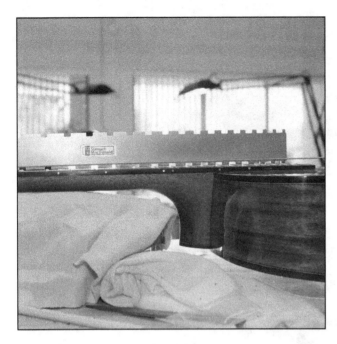

FIGURE 1.7.90. Once all the strings are on and tuned to pitch, we do a quick check of the "relief" in the neck. The relief is the amount of curvature in the neck. Note the light shining under the straightedge. In this case, it is approximately .012" high (not too bad). Relief is a desirable thing. When a string is plucked, it vibrates with a certain envelope. If the neck is dead straight, the vibrating envelope will cause the string to bottom out or buzz at some point along the fingerboard. Having the proper amount of relief helps lower the action to the best point, while allowing room for the string to vibrate without buzzing. The louder a player plays, the more relief, and higher action is needed. The softer he plays, the more action can come down; relief can be minimized but should not be eliminated.

FIGURE 1.7.91. To set the heights of the strings, we put a feeler gauge under the strings at the first fret and push the string down, touching the gauge. Note, we use a .010 gauge for the low E and A strings, a .009 for the D and G strings, and a .008 for the B and high E strings.

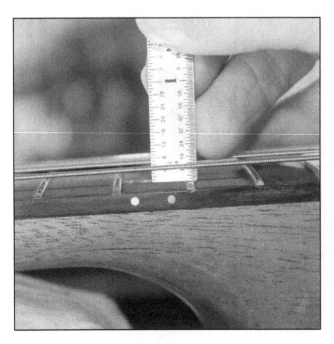

FIGURE 1.7.92. To measure the low E string, we hold the string down against the feeler gauge at the first fret and measure its height between the top of the twelfth fret and the bottom of the string as shown. In this case, we are just over 8/64". This will be uncomfortably high for most players, so we will plan to bring this number down to about 5/64", which we consider to be a little under average (but is requested by our customer).

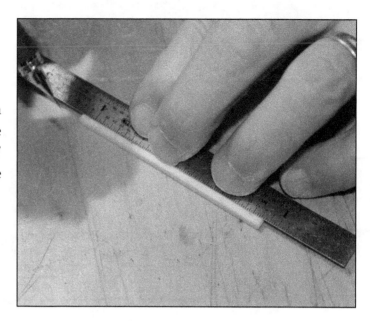

FIGURE 1.7.93. Since we need to take the action down by 3/64″ at the twelfth fret, we need to take the saddle down by double that amount or 6/64″ (3/32″). We mark this on the saddle and draw the line where we need to sand.

FIGURE 1.7.94. Once we have sanded the bottom of the saddle to the line on the disc sander, we put the saddle back into the saddle slot and mark between the strings (center the lines between the strings as closely as possible).

FIGURE 1.7.95. Next, we put the marked saddle into a small vise. Using our fine file, we file the saddle to a rounded point at the proper intonation point for each string. The points are filed as follows: the high E is filed to a point at the front edge of the saddle. The B string is filed to a point at the back edge of the saddle. Then an edge is filed diagonally from the front of the saddle for the G string to the back of the saddle for the low E string. Note: don't make the sadle points too sharp. Keep them slightly rounded. Sharp points will chip off.

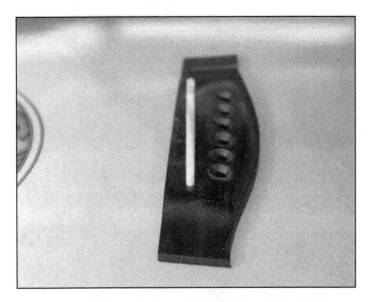

FIGURE 1.7.96. Here is a close-up of the saddle. Unfortunately, some of the photo is out of focus, but hopefully the basic idea of how the saddle is filed is clear.

FIGURE 1.7.97. Now that the saddle is shaped and is at the proper height, we focus on the nut. First, hold the nut file so that you can easily file the same angle every time. If you hold your hand at a random height above the strings, you cannot be sure. We like to put the file over a finger as shown. Then that finger will be moved along the top of the strings to keep the file at a constant angle. This also just happens to be the angle about halfway between the fingerboard and the headstock. This means that the string will rest solidly along the entire length of the nut file slot, which is what you want.

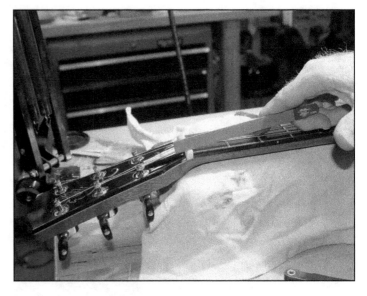

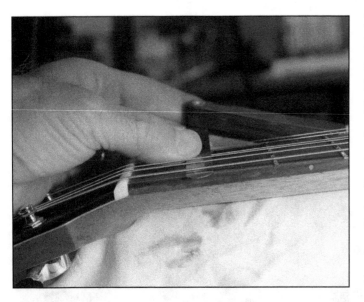

FIGURE 1.7.98. After filing the slot for the low E string, you can see that we're leaving the string a little high above the .010 feeler gauge—just a little. You definitely would rather be just a little high than a little low in this case.

This process is repeated for each string (as mentioned before, use the .010 gauge for the low E and A, the .009 gauge for the D and G, and the .008 gauge for the B and high E string and leave each one a little high over the gauge).

That's about it. The next step is to take the guitar for a test drive.

FIGURE 1.7.99. Fantastic—at least that's my opinion. We'll get a pickguard put on and call our customer to get his opinion.

FIGURE 1.7.100. Here is Tony Seale, who ordered this guitar. The story of this guitar is an interesting one. Tony first came into the shop with a vintage Gibson J-45, which he had just bought from one of the large chain guitar stores in the Phoenix area. He wanted me to appraise the guitar and let him know if he had gotten a reasonable deal. He could still return the guitar if he decided he didn't want it. I looked it over, and it definitely didn't look right. It was old (or looked old), but the way the neck was carved didn't look like a professional company had made it (despite the fact that it had what looked like a real Gibson label). I did some checking on the web and found that the bindings on the guitar were the wrong color for the age the guitar was supposed to be. I decided to call my friend, John Greven, who has done a lot of repairs on vintage Gibsons, and described the guitar to him. He agreed that the guitar was not a Gibson and was a fake. I told Tony about my findings and my discussion with John and let him know what was wrong with the guitar. He decided to return it and get his money back. However, he decided to check out the guitars in my shop and liked our guitars. He decided to order one. It was a real pleasure working with Tony. He came by from time to time to check on his guitar, and I always enjoyed it when he stopped by. He ordered a Tor-Tis pickguard and wanted a little purple seal inlaid into it. I called John Greven again, ordered the pickguard from him, and told him I was going to inlay the seal into it. John told me to send him the seal, and he flowed the pickguard right around the seal—which turned out better (and easier) than an inlay. Thanks to John for a great job, and thanks to Tony for the order. It was the perfect guitar to put into this book.

PART 2:
THE ARCHTOP GUITAR

DRAWING 2.1.1 The Archop Guitar

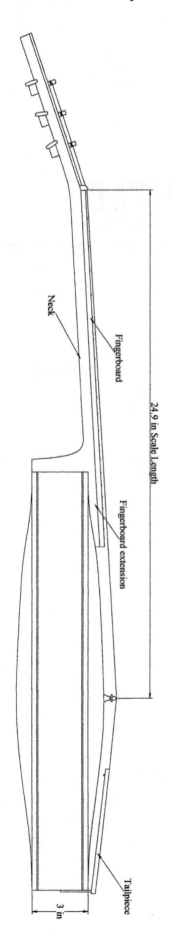

Neck

Fingerboard

24.9 in Scale Length

Fingerboard extension

Tailpiece

3 in

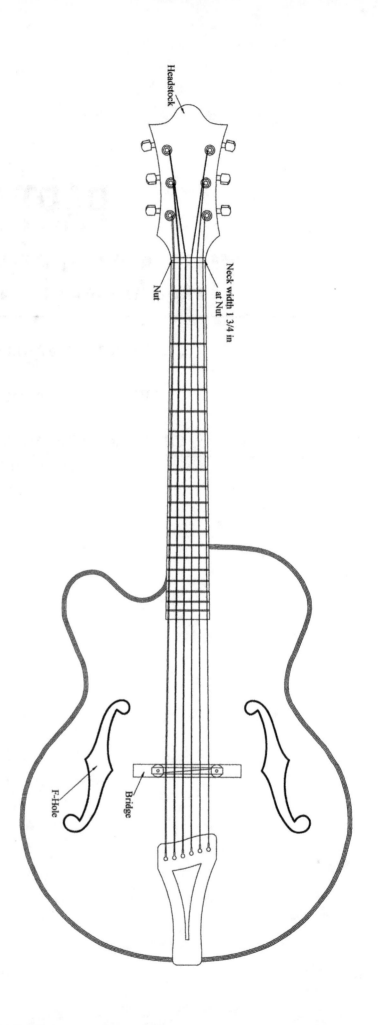

Headstock

Neck width 1 3/4 in at Nut

Nut

F-Hole

Bridge

DRAWING 2.1.2 The Archtop Guitar Braces

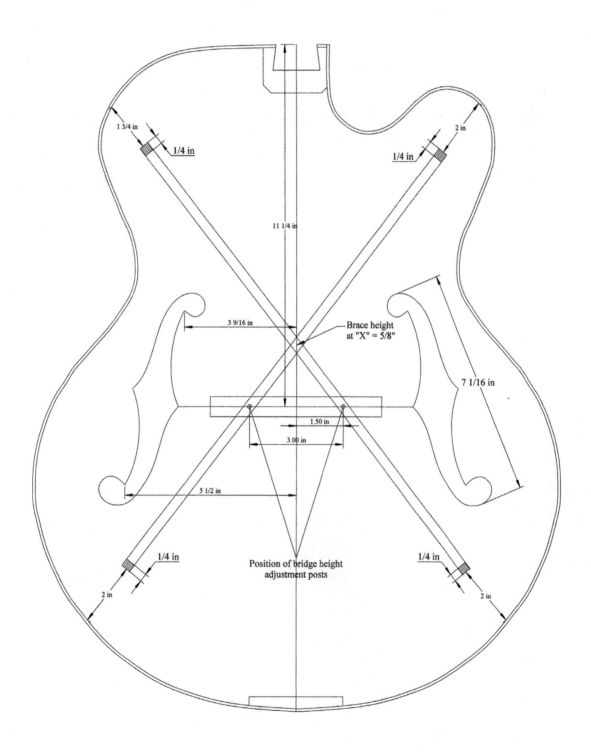

2.1
THE ARCHTOP BODY

THE ARCHTOP TOP AND BACK

In this section of the book, we will describe the construction of a carved top, carved back archtop guitar. We will focus on the steps that are different from those of the steel string guitar construction. You will see that many of the steps are the same, or very similar.

FIGURE 2.1.1. First, the desired arch for the top and back of the guitar must be designed. All dimensions must be accurate, and the curve of the arch should be smooth and graceful. As can be seen from the photo, the lower bout as well as the waist and upper bout must be planned. Leave nothing to surprise. We've been contacted many times by hobbyist first-time archtop builders who have bought expensive wood and started carving without a drawn plan, only to find that their dream guitar is a pile of scrap. The sketches shown in the photo show the arch across the lower bout and the waist; however, a sketch should also be made that shows the length of the guitar body and just how the builder wants the profile to look.

FIGURE 2.1.2. Here, two wedges of Sitka spruce being glued together in a simple jig comprised of a flat board and four pipe clamps. We have cleaned away the glue squeeze-out along the top of the glue joint and placed a couple of twenty-five-pound bags of lead shot on top to keep the boards level as pressure is applied by the clamps. We have also used this jig on many occasions to glue flat boards. The same procedure is used for the back of the guitar, but we are only going to show the process on the top.

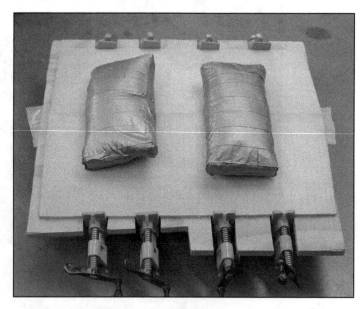

FIGURE 2.1.3. The completed rout plan, being transferred to the guitar top by tracing the drawing using carbon paper. Note that this is going to be a left-handed archtop.

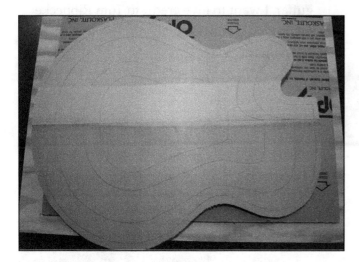

FIG 2.1.4. Here the rout plan is drawn onto the guitar top. Now, it is time to route the levels into the top.

FIGURE 2.1.5. In this photo, the rout is being done using an overhead pin router (pin removed for this job). It is critical that the board be pushed along *against* the direction of the router bit. If you go (just for a second) with the direction of the bit, the bit can grab your work and pull it (causing a tear, or worse, pulling your hand into the spinning bit). Therefore, keep your hands away from the bit and very carefully carve a little at a time until you get to the lines. Patience is required for this step. In the case of the archtop we are making, the lowest three levels are each 1/4" thick, and the top level is 1/8" thick, making the total thickness 7/8". Many archtops are designed with a higher arch

and many with a lower arch, but our customer wanted this arch after feeling several of our other guitars.

Note: It is not necessary to buy an overhead pin router, though if you plan to build many archtops, it is a very good way to go. Something similar can be handmade and will work very well.

After the arch levels have been routed, we use an angle grinder (Figure 2.1.6 and 2.1.7), with 24-grit paper to do the initial leveling and carve of the arch. The table has a downdraft section that pulls the work piece down, holding it in place, while most of the sawdust is pulled into the vent on the side. We recommend that you try this carving technique with some inexpensive material first to get the feel for the equipment rather than risking expensive wood for trial and error. Gluing a couple of pieces of 2 x 8 pine and shaping a test top can give you a great feel for the job.

FIGURE 2.1.6. It takes a few strokes of the grinder to get the feel of carving away the sharp edges, but this is the main trick to carving the top and back of the archtop guitar. I want to give credit to Tom Ribbecke for giving permission to discuss this technique in the book.

FIGURE 2.1.7. Here is another view of the process. Notice how the dust is swirling into the dust collector vent. It is critical to have good dust collection for a step like this.

FIGURE 2.1.8. Since the angle grinder is very aggressive, we will switch over to a random orbital palm sander using about 60-grit paper to remove the remainder of the ridges after the grinder has gotten them very low. As the ridges continue to get smoother, we will switch to 100 grit, then move to 150. This is smooth enough for now, since final sanding will be done with 220, and we are not yet ready for that.

FIGURE 2.1.9. After sanding, look at the surface of the top in the light and look for bumps and shadows. In Figure 2.1.10, we have placed a steel ruler on the top, and you can see that the shadows are very symmetrical on each side. We're about done with this step.

FIGURE 2.1.10. In preparation for carving the underside of the top, we set up the drill press. Note there is a 5/16″ peg sticking up vertically in the base board. The right angle helps get the 5/16″ drill bit perfectly aligned (as close as possible) over the peg.

FIGURE 2.1.11. Since we're going to carve the top to be 1/4″ thick, we will use a brass setup block and set the drill to stop at exactly 1/4″ above the peg.

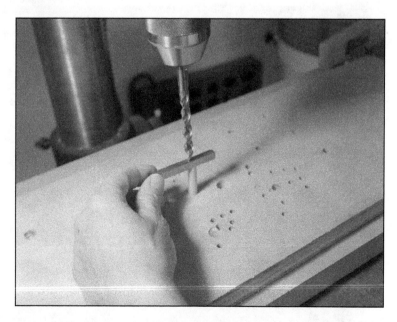

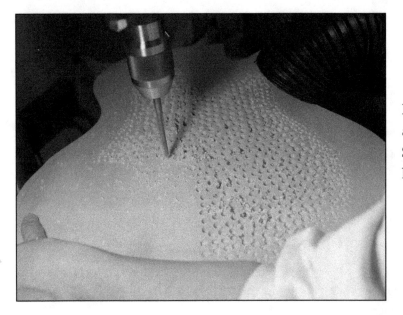

FIGURE 2.1.12. Next, a few hundred holes are drilled into the top, from the back side. Since the drill press has a depth stop, all the holes stop 1/4″ from the top surface.

FIGURE 2.1.13. Here is the underside of the top, ready for carving.

Note that after performing this step, the peg used in the drill press setup, which has been pressed against the top for each hole drilled, has left some slight dents in the top. These are nothing to worry about and will easily sand out.

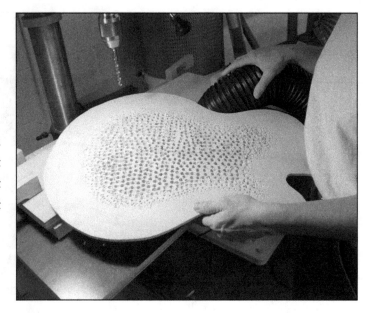

FIGURE 2.1.14. This is our work board. It is used to hold the archtop body around the edges and allows the arch to go in the recessed area. It is a critical part of building our archtops and is used in several steps.

It's worth the time and effort to make one work board for each size archtop you want to make.

FIGURE 2.1.15. Here is the top, clamped into the work board and ready for carving.

FIGURE 2.1.16. Now, as before, the angle grinder is used to take away the bulk of the excess. During steps like this, a lot of dust and wood chunks are thrown about (not to mention that an angle grinder along with a dust collector makes a lot of noise), so proper dust, eye, and ear protection must be used. Once the sanding gets close to the bottom of the drilled holes, switch from the angle grinder to the random orbital sander, just as we did on the top side above (see figure 2.1.8)

FIGURE 2.1.17. Here is the fully carved top. We check the thickness, and any areas are too thick, they are marked and either sanded or scraped down. This is another time that we will hold the underside of the top in the light to see if there are any shadows that show an uneven surface. Any traces of unevenness must be smoothed out prior to gluing braces to the top.

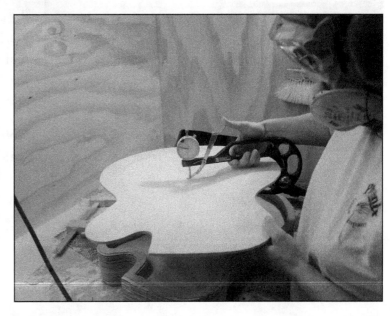

CREATING THE ARCHTOP F-HOLES

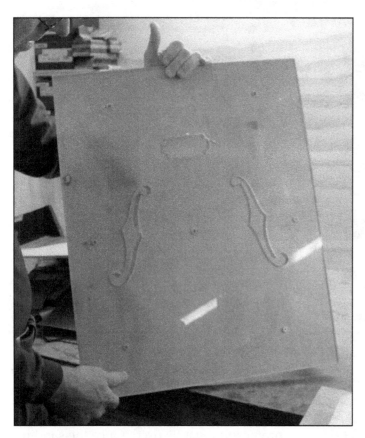

FIGURE 2.1.18. Now, we prepare for cutting the F-holes and the pickup hole. The jig shown was made for this purpose. It uses the pin in the overhead pin router. The top will be clamped to the side of the jig opposite the holes, and the pin will follow the holes. The router cuts directly above the pin.

FIGURE 2.1.19. The top is being clamped into the jig. It must be aligned to marks on the jig. First the centerline must line up, and second, you must mark where the bridge will go on the top (for our scale length, it is approximately 11 1/4" from the mark at the heel to the bridge. Note that this is also where the inner points of the F-holes are.

Note that this measurement is only good for a scale length of 24.9". If you wish to have a longer or shorter scale length, the measurement will have to change.

See the drawing below showing the measurements for an archtop.

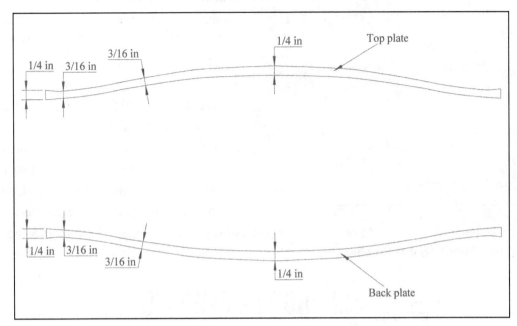

DRAWING 2.1.3 The Top and Back Profiles

FIGURE 2.1.20. Here is a close-up of the pin router making its cut. The pin is the same size as the cutter (1/4″ in this case), and the cutter is a down-cutting spiral. This causes the least amount of tear-out in the top as it cuts. Note that the entire depth of cut is not made in one pass. We cut about 1/16″ per pass until through.

FIGURE 2.1.21. Here is the final cut of all the holes. This is a very dirty job. Notice all the sawdust on my shirt. This is the reason I use a 3M Breathe Easy system, since it has a good face shield and blows filtered air through the helmet. This also keeps the shield from fogging up. I'll usually keep this on until I've vacuumed myself off and have gotten most of the dust away from the area. We also have smaller, simpler face dust filters for jobs that don't generate as much dust.

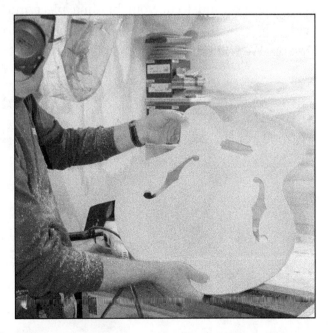

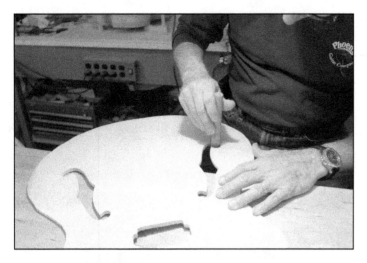

FIGURE 2.1.22. After cutting the holes, some tear-out has to be removed. In addition, we want to sharpen the rounded corners of the F-holes. We will use several sizes of files and little homemade sanding jigs, like the one shown. This is made from a dowel and flattened on one side. It is perfect for most of the sanding of the F-hole. You want the edges of the holes to remain perfectly vertical—as they were right after they were originally cut. You will minimize the tear-out by being sure that your router bit is fresh. It's not worth it to continue to reuse a worn bit because the work to clean up the holes will continue to be more difficult. A bit can last a longer if you can keep it clean and use a solution like Trend Tool & Bit Cleaner.

BINDING THE F-HOLES

FIGURE 2.1.23. Now, it's time to bind the F-holes. Bound F-holes aren't on every archtop, but they seem to be on the finest ones, and they give the guitar a definite look of class. We're going to bind this guitar with three layers. The first, a black fiber layer .020 thick, is followed by maple (also .020 thick) and Indian rosewood, .025 thick for a total just over 1/16". We have measured one section of the F-hole using a piece of green masking tape and cut a fiber piece of the same size using an X-ACTO knife.

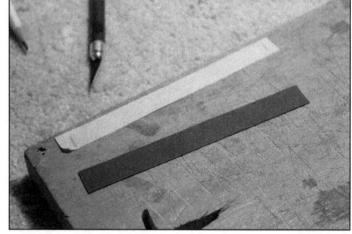

Note that you must cut your binding piece much wider than the thickness of the top, because the top is not flat, and the binding must follow the contour of the top. We will typically cut the piece about 1/2" wide to compensate.

FIGURE 2.1.24. The fiber is easy to bend, so just bend it around your finger and fit it into the F-hole. Then, using a white pencil (or any pencil that will show up on the black layer), mark the binding overlap as shown on both the top and back side of the guitar top.

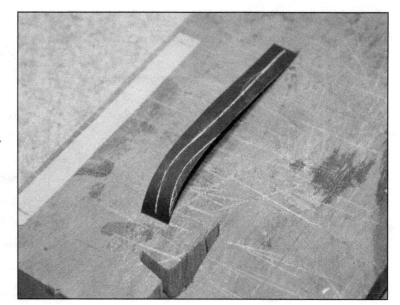

FIGURE 2.1.25. Here is the fiber piece, marked, ready to cut.

FIGURE 2.1.26. Scissors can be used to cut the fiber layer, but don't try this on the wood layers or they will split.

FIGURE 2.1.27. After the fiber has been cut, rebend the loop and apply glue. Don't use superglue in this case, or you risk the glue staining the light top a yellow color. We use Titebond for this step. If you use plastic bindings, Titebond may not be the best. There are good plastic glues for this. Note we have cut several strips of fiber tape ready to tape the binding down.

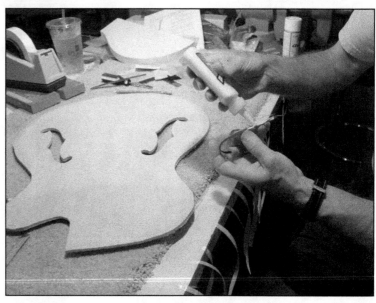

FIGURE 2.1.28. Once the binding has been put in place (with one side tightly against the corner of the F-hole, we use the tape to hold it in place. Note the overlap around the F-hole loop. We will cut this down to miter the joint later. When removing the tape, we never just pull it off—we use a small amount of naphtha, squirted from a pipette. This will allow the tape to pull off easily without tearing any of the soft wood fibers. It's best not to get any of the naphtha on your skin, so either use gloves or hold the tape with tweezers or small pliers to pull it up.

FIGURE 2.1.29. Once the two long legs of the F-hole (the ones with the loops) are bound and the glue is dry, sand them flush with the top and underside with sandpaper.

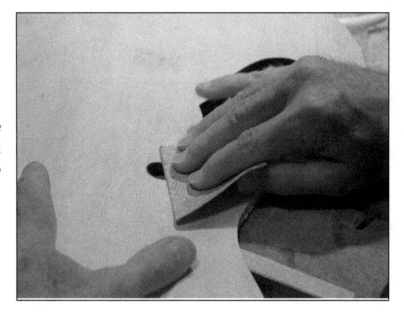

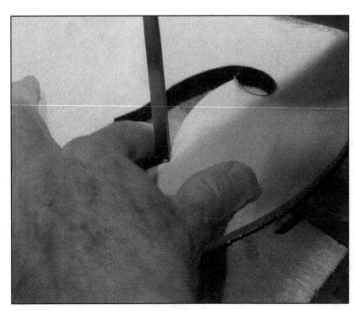

FIGURE 2.1.30. Once the binding is flush with the top and back, miter the corners and end of the loops with a sharp chisel.

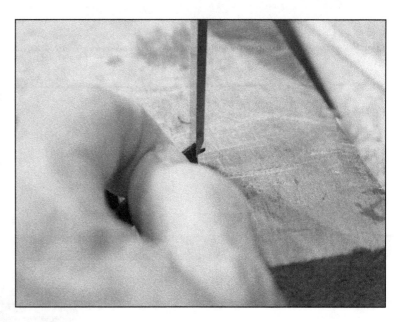

FIGURE 2.1.31. Prepare the short legs just as we did before, cut them to length, and carefully miter both ends with a chisel as shown. You may have to repeat this step a couple of times to get it just right—but it's worth it to get the fit you need.

FIGURE 2.1.32. Once the final fit looks good, go ahead and glue and tape the piece in place. When it is dry, sand everything flush with the top and back side of the top.

FIGURE 2.1.33. Once the black fiber layer is completed, it's time to work on the maple layer. First, cut the pieces to size as before, but then you must bend the maple on a hot iron. We use a spray bottle to wet the maple veneer, then heat it on the bender and curl it around a dowel. Be careful not to curl it too tightly too quickly, but this method will work very well. Then place the maple piece into the F-hole and mark it with a pencil—just as you did with the black fiber.

FIGURE 2.1.34. As mentioned above, don't try to cut the maple with scissors. Use a belt sander to sand away the excess and get down to the lines. Be sure not to sand your fingers during this step.

FIGURE 2.1.35. Here is the maple layer being taped over the black fiber.

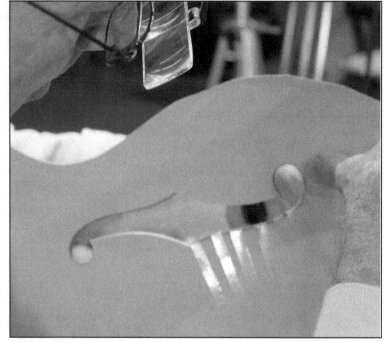

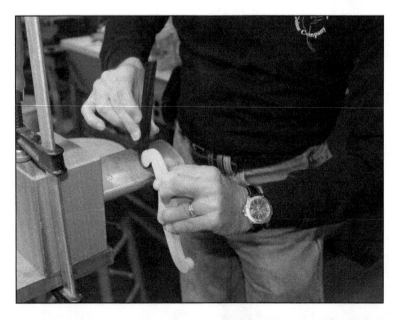

FIGURE 2.1.36. We use the same method for the initial bend on the Indian rosewood as we did above with the maple; however, we put this veneer into a homemade plywood caul the same shape but very slightly smaller than the actual F-hole. This caul will hold the veneer as it is shaped and cooled. You can see from this photo and the next that the curved end of the veneer fits into a small slot in the caul so it doesn't need anything special to hold it in place.

FIGURE 2.1.37. Once the veneer has been made pliable enough to bend around the caul, the free end is held down with a rubber band. After a few hours, it will be dried and will hold its shape well enough to be put into the F-hole so the contour of the hole can be drawn onto the veneer, and its final shape can be sanded down. This step helps keep the Indian rosewood from splitting.

FIGURE 2.1.38. Here is a close-up of the final F-hole binding. Indian rosewood was chosen as the outside layer because our customer wanted a very dark (Macassar ebony) binding on his guitar. The Indian rosewood looks very similar and is readily available in a veneer.

BRACING THE ARCHTOP GUITAR TOP

FIGURE 2.1.39. Here is the underside of the top. We have drawn a line between the inner points of the F-holes. This line shows the position where the bridge will go on the opposite side of the top when the guitar is complete. The X's show the position of the bridge posts (in this case, they are 3" apart, each 1.5" from the centerline of the guitar top). This guitar will have X braces, and they will be glued directly under the bridge posts. We like to keep the spread of the X as wide as possible, since that has a very direct impact on

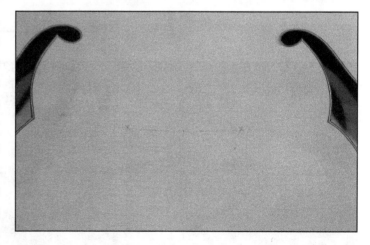

the tone of the guitar. The wider the spread, the mellower the tone will be. The narrower the spread of the X, the sharper and more brittle the tone will be. This is the same for parallel bracing. Since the separation of parallel braces is comparatively narrow, the tone also tends to be sharper than that of an X brace.

FIGURE 2.1.40. The brace wood should be quartersawn and about 1 1/4″ high and 1/4″ to 5/16″ wide. We run all our braces through our thickness sander to get them exactly how we want them before trying to use them. Next, each brace is placed down on the underside of the top, and their positions are carefully marked with a pencil so they can be placed back exactly where we want them, with no guesswork. If you look closely, you can see the mark in the lower left-hand corner of the photo showing the position mark of the next brace to be used. We are using a compass to follow the profile of the underside of the arch and mark it onto the brace. We will perform this same step with both braces. Note that the brace must be tall enough to be 1/4″ to 5/16″ tall at the end of the brace. The brace will be very tall in the center, where the curve of the top is deepest, but we will carve that brace down to be about 5/8″ tall where the braces meet at the X.

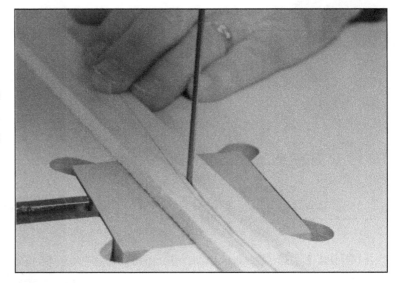

FIGURE 2.1.41. After marking with the compass, the brace is cut out on the band saw. Note that I am leaving plenty of space and not cutting too close to the line.

FIGURE 2.1.42. Here is the roughsawn brace placed into the top. The top is cradled in the work board where it will be clamped down, and the brace will be sanded to match the shape of the arch.

FIGURE 2.1.43. Now, we put two cam clamps on each end of the brace we want to work, so the brace aligns perfectly with the alignment marks we put onto the top. The remaining clamps are there for stability. Next, we take a piece of 80- to 100-grit sandpaper and put it under the rough brace with the sandpaper side up against the brace. We sand it until the face of the brace perfectly matches the surface of the arch. These two surfaces must match because they are about to be glued together, and we don't want any gaps between the surface of the brace and the surface of the top. It's a good idea to use a glove on the hand holding the sandpaper.

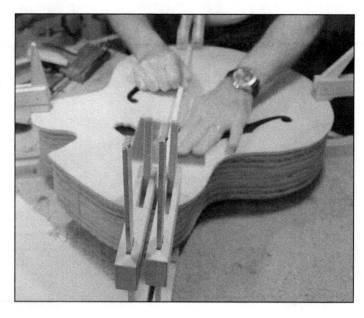

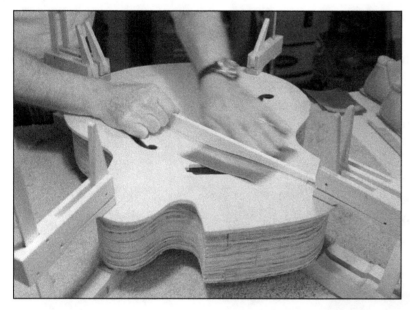

FIGURE 2.1.44. Here is another view of the brace being sanded. Note the notch on the far right (upper bout) side of the brace. This is put there to allow the sandpaper to get under the brace all the way to its end but still have an extension that can be held in place by the clamps. This extension will be sawed off after the brace is glued in place. Sand both braces to match the top profile.

FIGURE 2.1.45. Now it's time to carve the notch and fit the X together. The photo shows that we have put cam clamps to align both braces, so we can mark the intersection point of the X.

FIGURE 2.1.46. After the position of the X is marked on the lower brace, it is put into a vise, and we use a thin kerf saw to cut the edges.

FIGURE 2.1.47. Once the edges of the notch are cut, use a thin chisel to get rid of the center of the notch. Be sure you don't use the chisel below the level of the saw line—you'll split your brace.

We like to leave the height of the lower brace about 3/4 of the total height of the braces (not half). We feel that this gives a stronger brace at the X than if each brace is 1/2 the total height.

FIGURE 2.1.48. After the lower brace notch is done and at the right height, place the upper brace into the notch and mark on the side of the brace where it intersects with the lower brace.

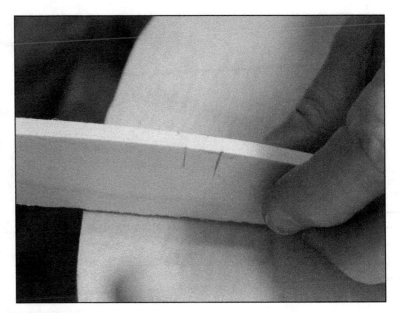

FIGURE 2.1.49. Here are the marks on the upper brace.

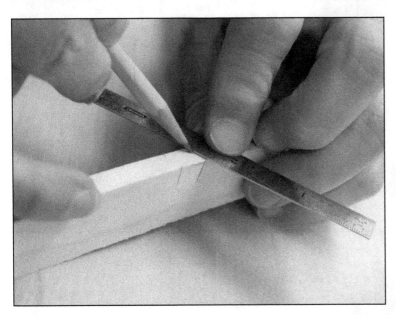

FIGURE 2.1.50. Now, transfer the points from each side of the brace and cut the notch as before. Since this is the upper brace, it will be much thinner over the notch than the lower brace; therefore, you will have a much deeper cut than before.

FIGURE 2.1.51. Here is the X brace, all fit together and ready for gluing.

FIGURE 2.1.52. Here are the braces with glue applied and the first clamp on. We have excellent squeeze-out almost the entire length of all the braces.

FIGURE 2.1.53. Clamps are all on. Note that on an archtop, you can see that the clamps do not sit evenly on the bench. We put small wedges or sometimes other clamps under these "floating" clamps, to keep them from causing stress on the top during a glue-up.

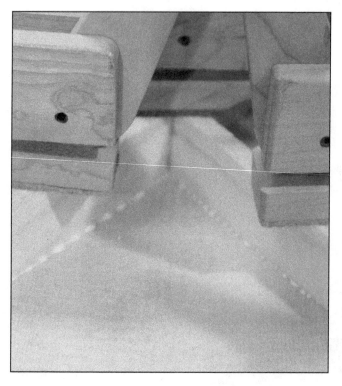

FIGURE 2.1.54. Here is a good close-up of the glue squeeze-out right after clamping. This has to be cleaned up. It's best to wait for a few minutes (maybe ten or so), until the glue has slightly gelled so it will clean up more easily. You can start cleaning right away, but the job is more difficult.

FIGURE 2.1.55. We use a small tool for clay sculpting for cleaning up glue. We buy them at an art supply shop. To get the squeeze-out on the other side of the braces, we must carefully go between the clamps to get the excess glue.

FIGURE 2.1.56. After the glue is dry, we cut off the extensions of the braces and measure exactly how tall we want the braces to be. This guitar is a 17″ (lower bout), so we will make the braces 5/8″ tall (at the X). For a smaller guitar, we will make the braces shorter.

FIGURE 2.1.57. The braces are carved with a small, curved-sole plane. Sometimes the spruce of the brace wants to chip and tear out as you carve. When this happens, turn the work around and go in the other direction. This will usually solve the problem.

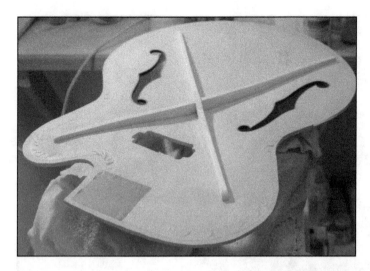

FIGURE 2.1.58. Here is the top, braces carved, in the spray booth ready for a seal coat of shellac. You can see that the rim of the top where it will glue to the guitar sides and kerf has been taped off as have the areas of the head block and tail block.

Note: We will not have a separate section on the archtop guitar back, since it is carved exactly like the top, only it does not have braces or F-holes.

THE ARCHTOP SIDES

We want to go into some detail about bending the archtop sides or any sides of highly figured wood. It is very common for figured woods to split during bending, so we will show how we help to prevent this from happening.

FIGURE 2.1.59. Two pieces of book-matched, flamed maple are the sides. We are marking the waist. The sides have been sanded down to about .085" thick.

FIGURE 2.1.60. A mark has been made on the cutaway side, about halfway between the waist mark and the outer point of the cutaway. We are thinning the section from this mark to the end of the cutaway down to about .065". First, we will put the side board into the sander. Then we will stop the sander and reverse the travel of the feed belt. When we take out the board, we will measure the thickness of the area we have sanded and repeat until we have the thickness we need.

FIG, 2.1.61. After we get the thickness of the maple side, we glue a thin veneer (in this case, a .020 thick veneer of walnut) to the thinned down portion of the maple side. In this photo, we are trimming the veneer after it has been glued. With the veneer, the total thickness of the side will be very nearly equal to that of the rest of the side.

FIGURE 2.1.62. In this photo, we show the Fox bender with a cutaway attachment. However, by adding the springs between the last two posts, the area of the inward cutaway is given much more protection against splitting, since the board fibers are held together. This technique, along with gluing the veneer to the cutaway portion of the side, significantly prevents splitting, even with highly figured woods. Thanks to Michael Baranik for this idea.

FIGURE 2.1.63. Here are the final bent sides, freshly out of the benders, and clamped into our molds.

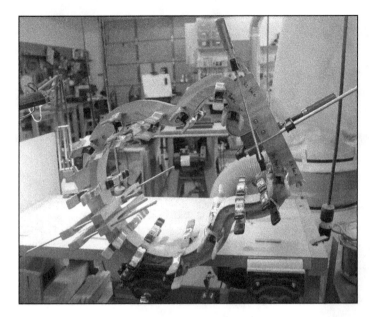

FIGURE 2.1.64. After the edges are trimmed, as we did in Figs. 1.3.11 and 1.3.12 for the steel string, we make the endblock and headblock and clamp them as shown.

FIGURE 2.1.65. Once the headblock and endblock are glued in, we first replace all the clamps with go-bars, just as we did with the steel string (and all of our guitars). We profile the edges of the sides with a flat sanding board. Then we start cutting kerf. We cut two identical pieces at a time as shown, using a cutting board to keep from damaging the bench.

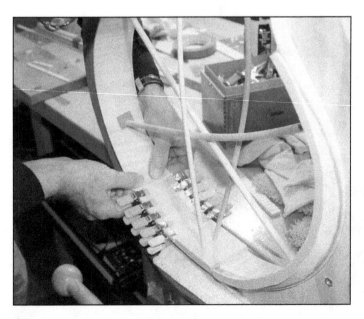

FIGURE 2.1.66. Here, the two lengths of kerf have been glued and clamped in, and we have cut a short piece of spruce (what we call a Popsicle stick) and get ready to glue it in perpendicular to the kerf. We always cut two identical pieces of kerf so we can glue the Popsicle sticks evenly around the side. The purpose of the Popsicle sticks is to stop a split in case the player hits his guitar, and the side starts to crack.

FIGURE 2.1.67. In this photo, the Popsicle stick is glued in with another Popsicle stick (used as a caul) and glue is cleaned up. This procedure is repeated until the kerf goes all the way around the edges of the top and back of the guitar. The spacing of the Popsicle sticks can vary. We tend to put them every 4 1/2" or so. We have also seen different luthiers put the kerf on in an unbroken string around the guitar, and then put Popsicle sticks between the top and back kerf. Either method is OK.

At this point, we will reprofile the sides (see Figs 1.3.24 and 13.25) using a flat sanding board. Then we will align the top and back to the sides, in a similar way that we did with the steel string, except this job is much easier since we don't have to tie any braces into the kerf. We just need to be sure the top and back are properly centered from side to side and that the points of the F-holes are exactly 11 1/4" from the end of the headblock.

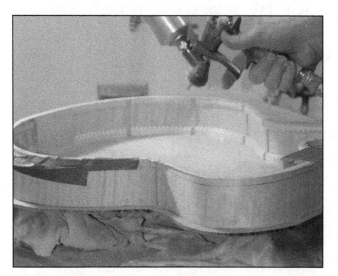

FIGURE 2.1.68. Here is the archtop, with the sides done and the kerf and Popsicle sticks in place. The back has been glued on (using the same method we used in gluing on the back of the steel string), and we're spraying the back with shellac. The top of the kerf is taped off (as are the tops of the endblock and headblock). We have also taped off the bevel to keep it clean. We're not going into the making of the bevel in this book, but two of three guitars being made in this book have them because our customers ordered them that way. Note: spraying a wash coat of shellac is typically done on archtops, since after carving, you are left with a lot of open grain.

FIGURE 2.1.69. Here is the completed archtop body, after binding. We are not going into the binding steps here because they are identical to the binding of the steel string guitar. We use the same jig to hold the guitar and cut the binding slots and glue and strap the binding on in the same way. That's part of the purpose of this book—to show that most of the steps involved in building each of these very different types of guitars are very similar (or identical).

FIGURE 2.1.70. This photo shows using a curved scraper to carve the recurve. Drawing 2.1.3 shows what the recurve should look like. The groove made by the scraper must be smoothed out to look like the natural curve of the arch before final sanding is done. Note that if you are making an acoustic archtop, the recurve can be deeper, helping the top to flex farther. However, if you are making a guitar that will be played with a pickup, the recurve cannot be as drastic, or the guitar is likely to have a feedback problem. That is why we show the minimum thickness in the recurve area as being 3/16″, since this guitar (and most of the archtops we make) will have a pickup. We have found this recurve thickness to have a very pleasant acoustic tone (and add significant acoustic tone to the amplified sound) without a significant feedback issue. Note that you can always make an amplified instrument feedback with too much volume or if you're too close to the amp.

2.2
THE ARCHTOP NECK

The archtop neck starts out the same way as the steel string neck, with the possible exception of the scale length. The typical scale length of the archtop necks that we have made has been 24.9", but we have had other scale lengths ordered. Figs 1.4.1 through 1.4.47 in the steel string neck chapter are the same, so they will not be reviewed again in this chapter. We will start at the point where the neck dovetail has been cut, and the "ears" have been glued onto the sides of the headstock. Realize that one major difference between the steel string neck and the archtop neck is the angle at which the neck is held in the jig as the dovetail is cut. The steel string neck angle is 1.5 to 2 degrees. The archtop neck is about 4 degrees. You must have an accurate drawing to determine your neck angle, because it is dependent upon the height of the arch carved into the top.

FIGURE 2.2.1. This is the first step to make the fingerboard extension. A piece of wood from the leftover neck material scrap is chosen for the extension. It is cut to approximate length (about 6") and is sanded to 1/2" thick for this guitar. This archtop has a built-in pickup. If this had been an acoustic archtop or if it had a floating pickup, the fingerboard extension would be thicker (about 5/8"), therefore making the fingerboard sit higher off the body of the guitar. In this case, we want the strings to be closer to the body and the built-in pickup.

FIGURE 2.2.2. The router table is set up with a wide bit (5/8") at a depth of 1/2".

FIGURE 2.2.3. Next, the slot is cut into the end of the fingerboard and dovetail for the fingerboard extension. Note that we do not make the whole cut at once. We only cut about 3/16" at a time to keep the cut very smooth. We will end up cutting about 1/4" beyond the dovetail into the fingerboard itself.

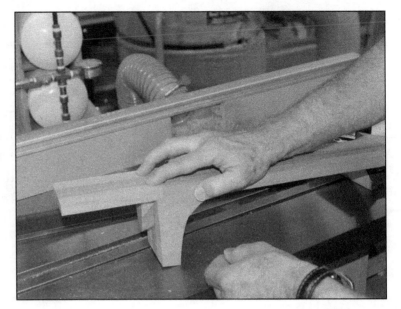

FIGURE 2.2.4. Here we see the fingerboard extension as it is fitted onto the slot in the fingerboard and dovetail.

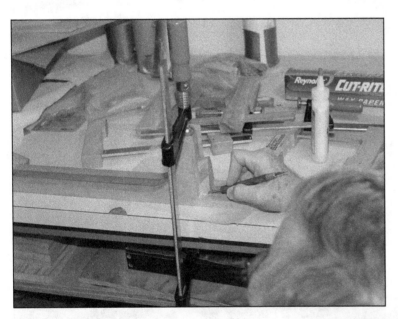

FIGURE 2.2.5. The glue-up for the fingerboard extension is very simple—don't forget to put some wax paper under the glue joint and clean up the squeeze-out.

FIGURE 2.2.6. Once the fingerboard extension is glued on, the truss rod will no longer fit, so we will put the truss rod into the slot and mark the end of the new slot with a pencil.

FIGURE 2.2.7. The laminate trimmer is set to the same depth as the truss rod slot and is carefully guided by hand until it is the proper length. Then the rounded end of the slot will be squared off with a chisel, until the truss rod fits properly into the slot.

FIGURE 2.2.8. Here is the neck, ready for the fingerboard to be glued. The truss rod is in the slot, with a thin strip of maple glued to the top of the truss rod. Both carbon fiber rods have been glued into their slots, and the top of the neck has been sanded flat, so it is ready for the fingerboard glue-up.

At this point, the fingerboard glue-up is the same as the glue-up of the steel string fingerboard, except that the steel string fingerboard overhangs the neck and glues directly to the body (in the case we are describing in this book). However, for our archtop, the end of the fingerboard glues to the fingerboard extension, and the fingerboard extension is glued to the top of the guitar.

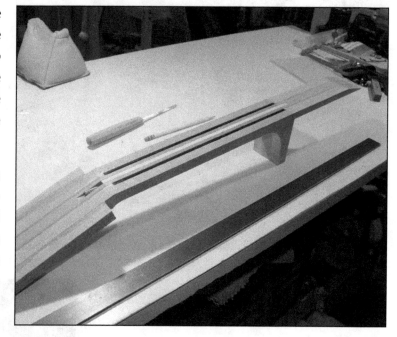

After the fingerboard is glued, the headstock laminate is glued, and the headstock and neck are trimmed as they are with the steel string. The main difference here is that the archtop headstock is typically much larger than the typical steel string headstock. This is mainly due to tradition.

FIGURE 2.2.9. Now we are going to focus on the fit of the neck to the body of the guitar. Here, we draw a line defining the "shoulders" of the neck heel. We will chisel out material between the shoulders and the dovetail to make the neck fit easier, rather than trying to fit the entire surface area of the heel to the guitar. The width of the shoulders should be about 1/8".

FIGURE 2.2.10. Here is the chisel making its initial score to carve out the material between the dovetail and the shoulders.

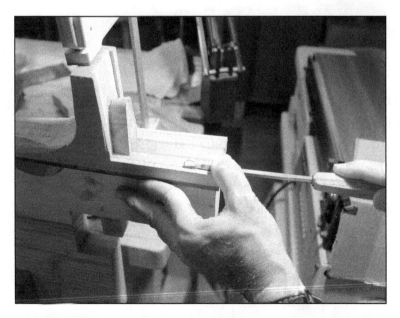

FIGURE 2.2.11. Now we will do the same thing to the underside of the fingerboard extension, for the same reason. We only want to fit the shoulders to the guitar top, rather than the entire surface of the fingerboard extension.

FIGURE 2.2.12. Now we start fitting the neck to the body. Put the neck dovetail into the body dovetail, and using a small compass, let the point of the compass follow the guitar top profile, while the pencil draws the profile onto the fingerboard extension.

FIGURE 2.2.13. Now we use a chisel to carve away the material up to the pencil line. This makes for an initial fit of the neck. We will now take care of a couple of other items before the final fit is complete.

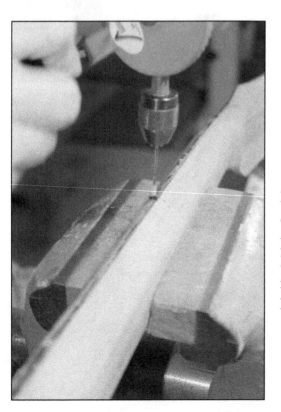

FIGURE 2.2.14. For the steel string guitar, we used 2 mm MOP dots for the fingerboard side dots. In this case, we are using plastic dots cut from a small plastic rod with a 1/16" diameter. Note the masking tape on the drill bit as a stop marker. After measuring the position for each of the side dots, we drill a 1/16" hole approximately 1/8" deep.

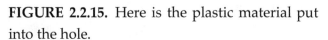

FIGURE 2.2.15. Here is the plastic material put into the hole.

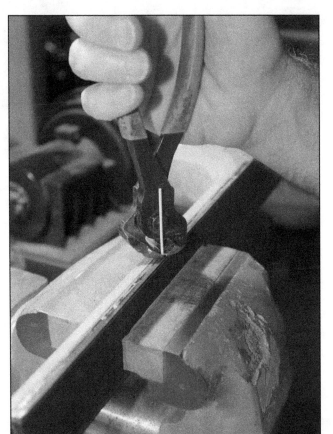

FIGURE 2.2.16. Cut off the plastic rod flush with the fingerboard edge.

FIGURE 2.2.17. Once all the dots are put in, they are glued, and we use a sanding block to level them. Note that since we are using dark bindings, we can use superglue. However, if we were using maple or other light wood for the bindings, we recommend using a drop of Titebond to hold the dots.

FIGURE 2.2.18. Here is the neck. You can see the side dots, and the fret markers have been inlaid.

FIGURE 2.2.19. Now we start aligning the neck and finish the fit. We check left to right alignment to the centerline (drawn on the top of the guitar), and we check alignment up and down (the neck angle) by measuring the plane of the neck with a straightedge as shown and by measuring the height of the straightedge above the guitar body at the point of the bridge (between the points of the F-holes). This height should be about 3/4" at this point. This is the measurement for the height measured when the pickup is built in. For a floating pickup, the measurement is closer to 1".

FIGURE 2.2.20. It the fit is close, and you can use sandpaper to make slight moves to the angles up/down or left/right. If you have a bad fit, you may need to use a chisel on the shoulders to make the angle right. Notice we have not yet put on the heel cap. The neck fit must be good before we do our heel cap, due to the critical nature of the measurements involved.

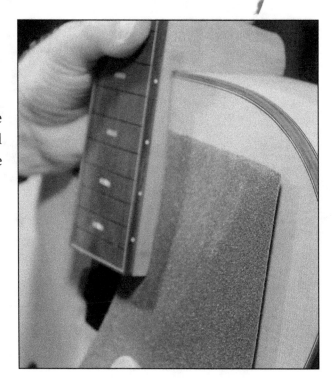

FIGURE 2.2.21. We also pull sandpaper to make the final fit on the fingerboard extension. Both the heel and the fingerboard extension must fit just right to the guitar body.

FIGURE 2.2.22. Here is the neck, put into our jig for cutting the heel in preparation for the heel cap. We are using the chisel to check when the alignment mark is directly aligned with the top of the jig (just as we did with the steel string heel cap cut).

Note the jig is angled, and this angle matches the angle of the neck, so the heel comes off the guitar side at a 90-degree angle.

FIGURE 2.2.23. Here is the heel cap being glued down. Note the brads (the same type we use with the fingerboard) that hold the cap in place during gluing. These brads are placed so they are outside the area of the final heel, and the holes will be carved away. We also align the other side of the cap (that goes against the guitar) flush with the guitar side of the heel—though alignment is never absolutely perfect, and a few pulls of sandpaper are typically necessary to get the overall fit perfect. Also note the special caul made for this purpose that allows us to give pressure to the maximum area.

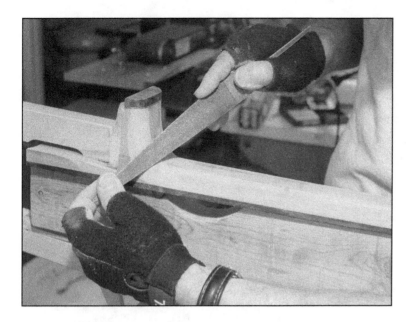

FIGURE 2.2.24. With the heel cap in place, we can complete the carving of the heel and the final fit of the neck to the body.

DRAWING 2.2.1 The archtop neck profile. Note that the profile is nearly identical to the steel string neck profile. The only difference is the radius of the fingerboard.

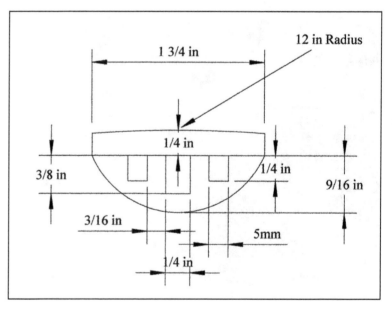

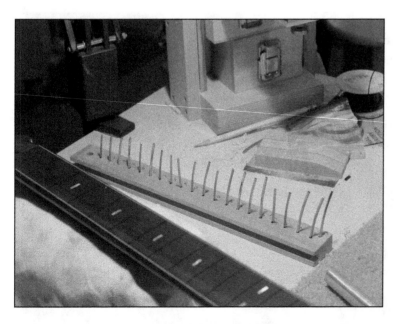

FIGURE 2.2.25. The archtop fingerboard is fretted off the guitar as opposed to the steel string guitar, which is fretted after the neck is attached to the body. There is no way to properly support the fingerboard extension for fret pounding once it is on the guitar.

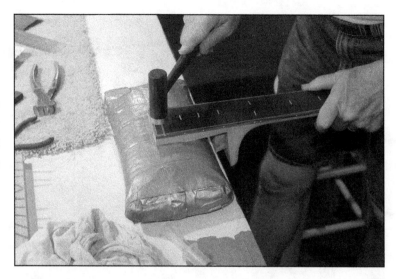

FIGURE 2.2.26. We use a bag filled with lead shot to stabilize the fingerboard extension as the frets are pounded in. For the rest of the neck, we will pound in the frets as we did for the steel string guitar.

FIGURE 2.2.27. Once the fret job is at this point, we will do the final neck fit, then glue on the neck of the archtop. We will also file the fret ends now. Fret leveling, crowning, and polishing will happen after the finish is applied.

Note that in this case, we are going to apply the finish with the neck on the guitar. It is also possible to finish the guitar just as we do the steel string—with the neck off the body. We are finishing this guitar with the neck on mainly because we are applying a very dark finish to the instrument, and we don't want any light spots appearing around the edges of the fingerboard. In the case of a natural or light finish, we will typically finish the body and neck separately.

PREPARATION FOR FINISH, FINISH SANDING AND BUFFING

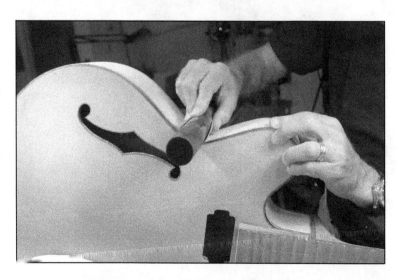

FIGURE 2.2.28. As with the steel string guitar, the body and neck are thoroughly sanded with 220-grit sandpaper prior to finishing. Note the fingerboard has been taped off.

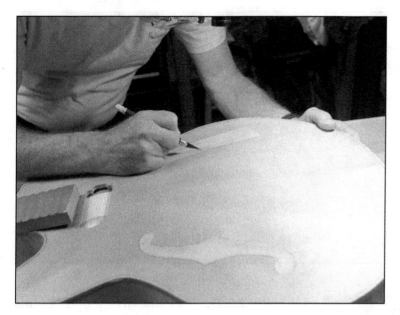

FIGURE 2.2.29. After all sanding is done, the surfaces not getting color are taped off. Note the tape covering all the bindings and purling as well as the fingerboard. We have taped the F-hole bindings and have blown up a balloon inside the pickup hole to keep finish from spraying into the guitar body. At this point, we will spray a few thin coats of color until the guitar is the correct shade. Then, we spray the same material and number of clear coats as the steel string finish.

After color is sprayed, the green detailing tape is removed so clear coats can be sprayed on the guitar, including the bindings. We will use a couple more balloons, one in each F-hole to keep spray from going into the guitar.

FIGURE 2.2.30. This photo shows the guitar being sanded after spraying. Due to the curved surfaces, we will usually sand an archtop by hand. However, the sanding schedule is the same as it was with the steel string. We'll start with 600- or 800-grit paper (wet sanding), depending on how smooth the surface is, and proceed to about 1200 before we start buffing.

FIGS. 2.2.31 AND 2.2.32. The sides and cutaway are also sanded by hand.

FIGURE 2.2.33. Here is the guitar being buffed, getting ready for final assembly

2.3
THE ARCHTOP BRIDGE, TAILPIECE, PICKGUARD, AND FINAL ASSEMBLY

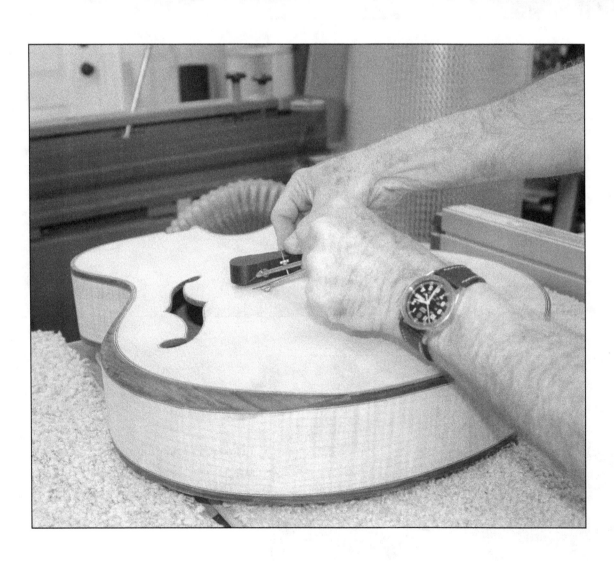

THE ARCHTOP BRIDGE

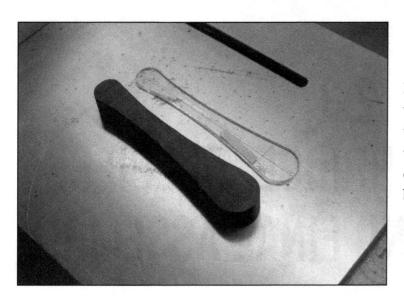

FIGURE 2.3.1. To make our archtop bridge, we start with our plastic template and draw the shape onto a piece of ebony about 5/8" thick. Then we cut close to the line and sand down to the line. We are left with a basic bridge blank as shown on in the photo.

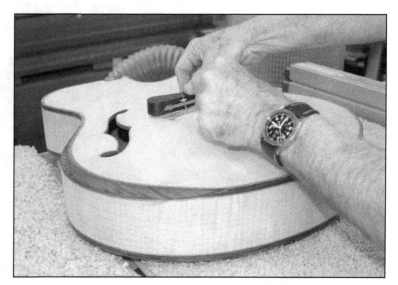

FIGURE 2.3.2. The bridge blank is placed between the points of the F-holes (very close to its final position), and a line is drawn on the blank with a compass, following the shape of the arch.

FIGURE 2.3.3. Here is a close-up of the shape we must carve into the base of the bridge. The bridge must be very snug against the top of the guitar.

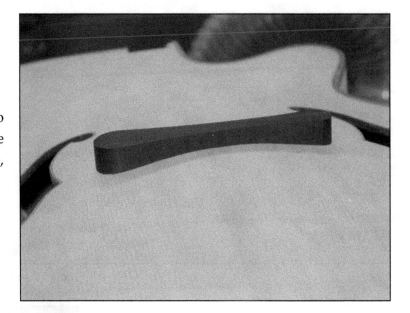

FIGURE 2.3.4. After using a band saw to cut just below the line, we can see that the bridge has a pretty close fit to the guitar top, but we have to make it fit exactly.

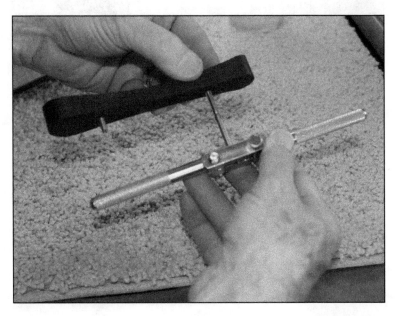

FIGURE 2.3.5. Now we must place the bridge posts. First, we establish a centerline on the bridge, then mark the posts 1.5″ on each side of the center. This will place the posts 3″ apart.

FIGURE 2.3.6. This photo shows the tap bit used to thread the postholes. A number 30 drill bit is used to drill the holes, then the holes are threaded with the tap, allowing us to thread the bridge posts into the holes. Do not drill the holes deep enough to go through the bridge.

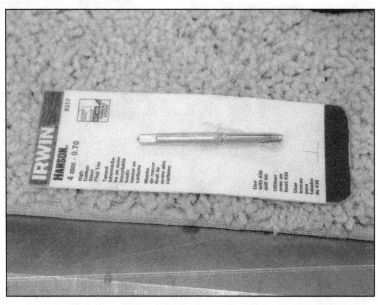

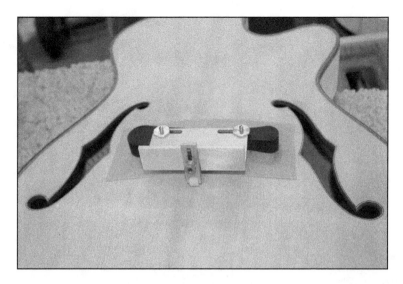

FIGURE 2.3.7. After the bridge posts are in, we use a piece of self-stick 120-grit sandpaper taped to the guitar top and a Stew-Mac archtop bridge fitting jig to sand the underside of the bridge to fit exactly to the top.

FIGURE 2.3.8. To shape the ends of the bridge, we use the same jig that we used to shape the wings of the steel string bridge. We simply let the radius of the belt sander wheel shape the wing of our archtop bridge. We'll have the new wing stop about 3/16" outside the bridge post-holes.

FIGURE 2.3.9. Once the wings are shaped, we put the bridge into a vise and taper the sides of the bridge. This makes the bridge look more streamlined and removes unnecessary weight.

FIGURE 2.3.10. Now we start working on the top of the bridge. First, prepare a piece of ebony about 1/2″ tall, 5/16″ thick, and 3 1/2″ wide. On the top, as shown in the photo, draw an arc of the same radius as the fingerboard (in this case, 12″) and sand the top to the drawn line.

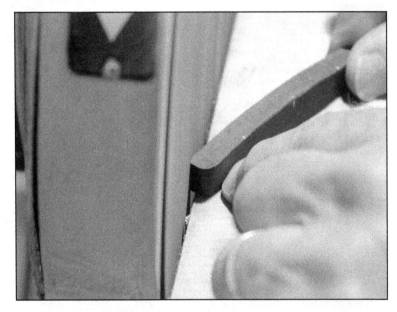

FIGURE 2.3.11. We use the disc sander to round the ends of the top of the bridge.

FIGURE 2.3.12. We now have to drill the holes in the underside of the bridge top. We will use a 5/32″ brad point bit. These holes must line up exactly with the holes in the bridge base, so the bridge posts will fit right in. We put tape on the drill bit to mark the depth.

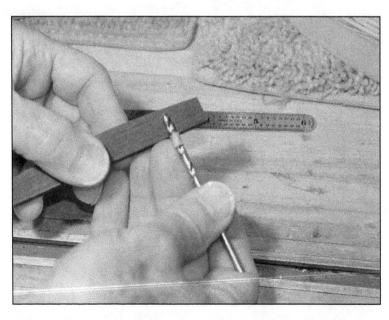

FIGURE 2.3.13. Now, we drill.

FIGURE 2.3.14. The lines are drawn on the top of the bridge top, showing where we want to carve away excess material, leaving the proper intonation points for our bridge.

FIGURE 2.3.15. The top of the bridge is being filed to shape. Note the white marks on the top of the bridge, marking where the strings will go. The spacing of the outside strings on this archtop is 2 3/16". The marks were made with the same Stew-Mac tool used to mark the string spacing on the nut on the steel string guitar.

FIGURE 2.3.16. Now, we must file a notch where we want each string to cross the bridge, which is marked by the white lines. We will use the same files that we use on the nut for the strings. Tilt the file so the string will intonate on the front edge of the slot.

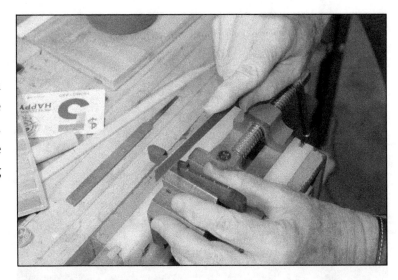

FIGURE 2.3.17. Here is a view of the final bridge that shows the carving on the top of the bridge for intonation.

THE ARCHTOP TAILPIECE

FIGURE 2.3.18. Our tailpieces are built around a stainless steel skeleton. We designed these pieces for a couple of reasons. First, we wanted to be sure that the tailpiece was strong. Even if the ebony gets dry and cracks, we want the tailpiece to hold. Second, we wanted to be able to ground the strings in case the guitar has a pickup (which is most of the time). We had our design built by a small manufacturing company and then had them powder coated.

FIGURE 2.3.19. We start with a piece of ebony about 1/4″ thick and big enough to trace the tailpiece skeleton.

FIGURE 2.3.20. After routing out the shape of the metal skeleton, we cut around the shape with the band saw.

FIGURE 2.3.21. After epoxying the metal skeleton into the ebony slot, we have the option to leave the bridge as a solid piece or to cut out the center and create a trapeze-style tailpiece. In this case, we are creating the trapeze-style tailpiece. We drill three holes in the corners and draw a line where we will cut with a coping saw.

FIGURE 2.3.22. We use a file to give the top of the tailpiece some definition and styling.

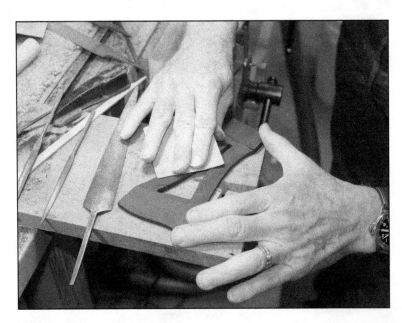

FIGURE 2.3.23. Once the shape is acceptable, we sand out all the tool marks.

FIGURE 2.3.24. Now we drill out the holes using a 3/16″ bit.

FIGURE 2.3.25. We now use a small saw to cut out the string slots. This is the same saw we used to cut the string slots for the steel string bridge.

FIGURE 2.3.26. A small file is used to widen and clean up the saw slots.

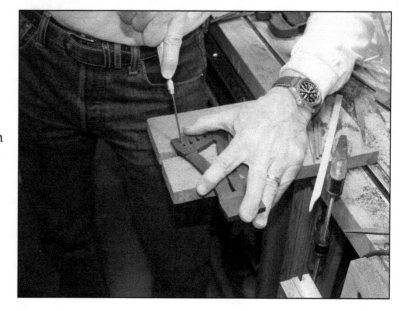

FIGURE 2.3.27. There it is—the nearly finished tailpiece. A couple more important things must be done before it is complete.

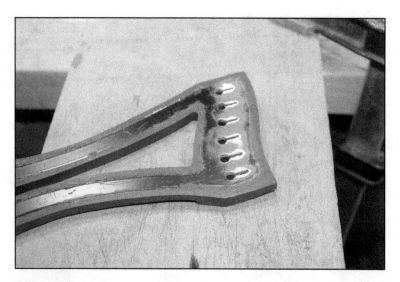

FIGURE 2.3.28. We have sanded off the powder coating where the balls of the strings will touch the bottom of the tailpiece. Earlier in this chapter, we mentioned that we designed this tailpiece so the strings could be grounded. This step and the next make that possible.

FIGURE 2.3.29. We also sand around the center screw hole on the other end of the tailpiece. As we screw on the tailpiece, we will wrap a small wire around this screw, connecting the other end to the housing of the output jack. You can see the wire attachment in Figure 2.3.40.

THE PICKGUARD

For this book, we will show our most popular pickguard rather than the one made for this guitar.

FIGURE 2.3.30. First, we take a piece of ebony, approximately 3/16″ to 1/4″ thick, and draw the outline of the pickguard from our template. Then, we band saw slightly outside the line, and using the belt sander, sand away the excess.

FIGURE 2.3.31. We then take a small block of ebony, about 1/2″ by 1/2″ by 1 1/4″, and glue it lengthwise on the pickguard blank as close to the small end as possible, with the edge directly on the edge of the pickguard that will fit against the fingerboard.

FIGURE 2.3.32. Next, we will use a block made for this purpose. It has a 3-degree bevel on the top edge. Some archtop pickguards come out from the fingerboard at a 90-degree angle. I find this uncomfortable and prefer the pickguard that tilts down slightly.

FIGURE 2.3.33. We use the angled block to sand the edge of the block (and the edge of the pickguard). With this angle sanded onto the edge, once the block is screwed to the fingerboard edge, the pickguard will angle down 3 degrees, making the fingerboard much more comfortable to use.

FIGURE 2.3.34. For the screws we are using, we drill through the block using a 3/16″ bit. Be sure the newly sanded edge is flat against the base so the rest of the pickguard is leaning at a 3-degree angle.

Drill two holes, at least 5/8″ apart.

FIGURE 2.3.35. Using a hand chamfer tool, we chamfer the edges of the holes so the screw heads will be flush with the block when screwed in.

FIGURE 2.3.36. Using the same size drill bit (in this case, a long aircraft bit), drill through the hole in the block, just scoring the surface of the fingerboard. We will use a smaller bit to actually drill out the screw hole in the fingerboard. We want the screw to pass easily through the block, but bite into the fingerboard.

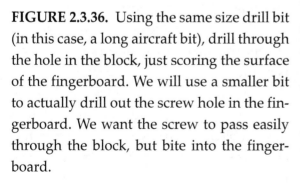

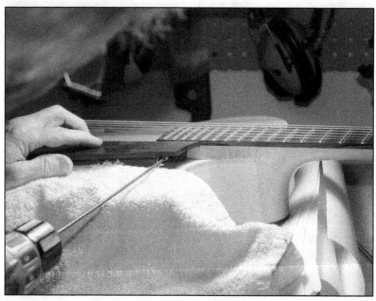

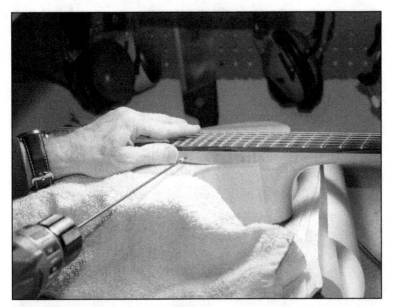

FIGURE 2.3.37. We now use a 1/8" aircraft bit to drill out the screw hole. The aircraft bit enables us to keep the drill far enough from the guitar to avoid scratches. Try to drill as straight as possible and perpendicular to the fingerboard edge. Note the tape on the bit, marking the depth.

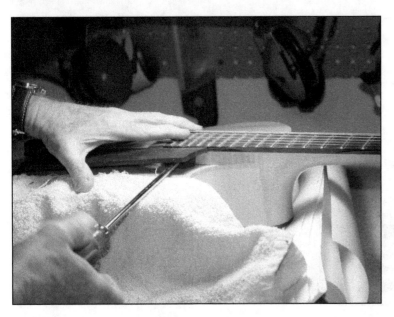

FIGURE 2.3.38. Finally, put in the screws. We found an extra-long screwdriver for this job.

FIGURE 2.3.39. Here is the final pickguard. Note how the pickguard angles down from the end of the fingerboard to the end of the pickguard. We like to install the pickguard after the neck is on the guitar and the strings are on. This way, we can make sure the angle is right. If the angle of the pickguard is too shallow, the edge of the pickguard is too close to the strings, and most players find this problematic. Also, note that from this angle you can see that the pickguard block has been sanded to an angle to match the angle of the arch of the top.

THE ARCHTOP FINAL ASSEMBLY

The pick guard is often part of our final assembly, but it can be done before finish if the guitar is to be finished with the neck on and is strung up in the white. If the guitar is finished with the neck and body separate, the final assembly is much like that of the steel string and the raised fingerboard classical in part 3. The frets are installed prior to finish, but the job of leveling, crowning, and polishing are done post-finish. The stringing and setup is done much like it was for the steel string, except the action for this guitar is much lower. At the first fret, the measurements are the same, but at the 12th fret, the height is approximately 3.5/64ths at the low E string, and 3/64ths at the high E string. In addition, it was mentioned in the section about the tailpiece that we use a wire to ground the strings. This is shown below in Fig 2.3.40.

FIGURE 2.3.40. Here is the connection to the tailpiece on the finished guitar. This will effectively ground the strings.

FIGURE 2.3.41. This is our good friend and the owner of the archtop made for this book, Jeff Libman. We has known Jeff for several years. He is an instrtuctor in the Department of Jazz Studies at Arizona State University, and holds a PhD in Music Education from ASU. He performs frequently in the Phoenix metropolitan area. It was an interesting challenge making a lefty guitar for Jeff. As are most professional players, Jeff is very particular about what he wants in a guitar. It is always a great learning experience making a guitar for a professional. We learn more

about neck profiles, neck relief, and just how low action can go. We thank him for trusting us with his guitar and hope Jeff will be happy with his guitar for a long time.

PART 3:
THE CLASSICAL GUITAR

DRAWING 3.1.1 The Classical Guitar

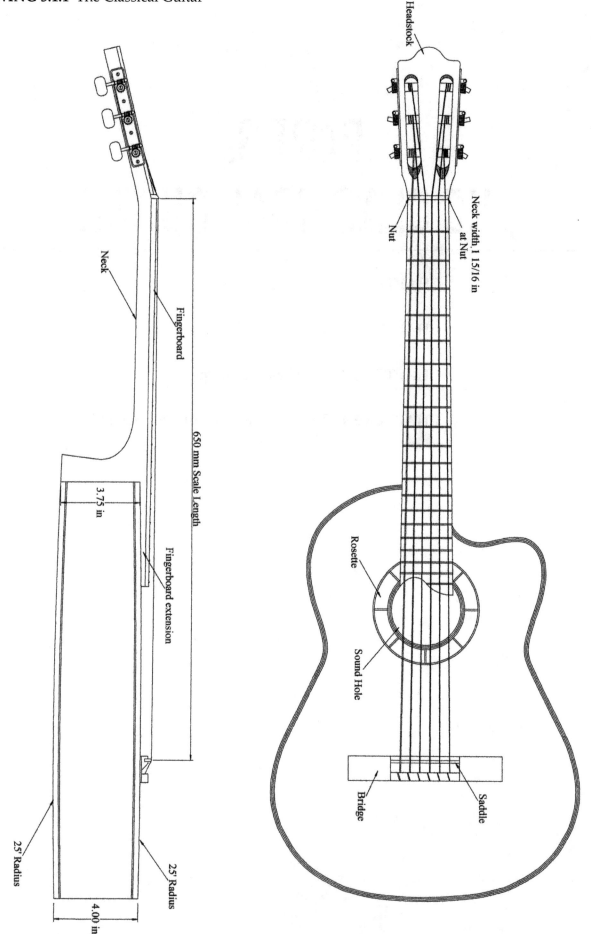

Headstock

Neck width, 1 15/16 in at Nut

Nut

Neck

Fingerboard

650 mm Scale Length

3.75 in

Fingerboard extension

Rosette

Sound Hole

25' Radius

25' Radius

4.00 in

Bridge

Saddle

DRAWING 3.1.2 The Classical Guitar Braces

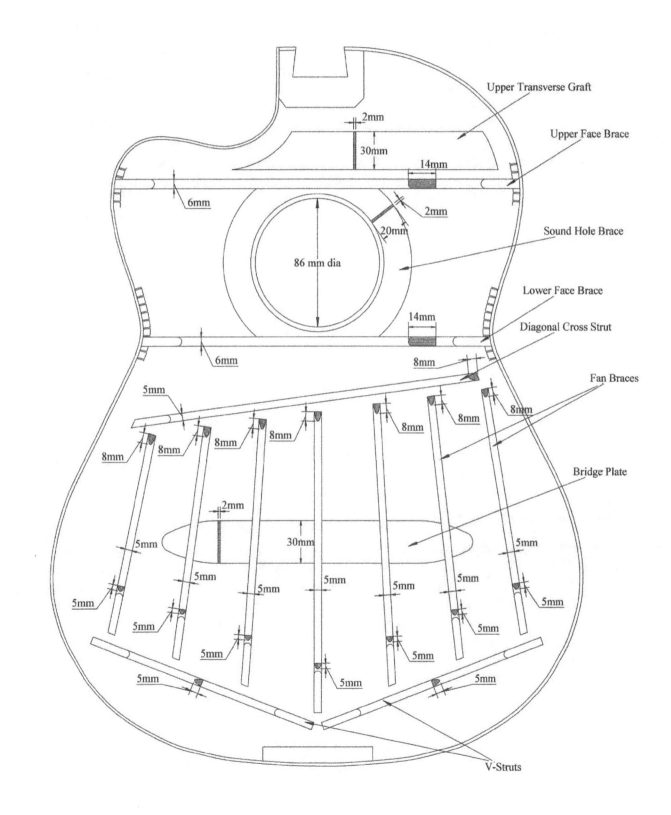

3.1
THE CLASSICAL GUITAR BODY

THE CLASSICAL GUITAR TOP

We start with a book-matched set of Engelmann spruce, glued together, and thickness sanded to approximately .150". At this point, we are ready to design the rosette.

FIGURE 3.1.1. For this rosette, our customer wanted a special design, somewhat in the style of Frank Lloyd Wright, so Diana created the design below.

FIGURE 3.1.2. The design shown is not a copy of any of Frank Lloyd Wright's designs; it is simply a design that is reminiscent of his style.

Clearly, this is not a traditional classical guitar rosette. For a good description of how to make a traditional classical rosette, see . Guitarmaking Tradition and Technology, by William R. Cumpiano and Jonathan D. Natelson.

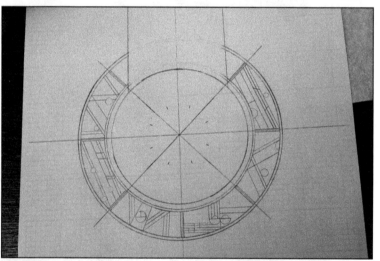

FIGURE 3.1.3. Here is a sample of some of the available inlay material, including Abalone (abalam), Mother-of Pearl, reconstituted stone, etc., and the different colors that we will use for various inlays, side dots, fret markers, etc. Our customer didn't want much abalone or MOP in this rosette.

FIGURE 3.1.4. The background material in the rosette will be Macassar ebony, thickness sanded to about 1/16″ (.062). The grain lines will be oriented in a radial direction on the rosette.

FIGURE 3.1.5. The Macassar ebony pieces are cut out slightly oversize using a jeweler's saw.

FIGURE 3.1.6. After measuring the inside and outside diameters of the rosette from the drawing, we make a couple of jigs like those used to make the steel string rosette. We first sand the inside radius on each rosette piece. Then, using the jig shown in the figure, we sand the outside radius. The final width of each piece will be 5/8″.

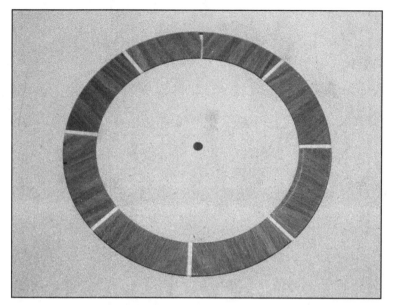

FIGURE 3.1.7. Here is the rosette base after each piece has been properly sanded to match at the edges. We put a 1/16" wide strip of maple between each of the Macassar ebony pieces except at the top of the rosette where the fingerboard will hide the rosette. The rosette is put into a 5/8" wide groove, cut into a piece of MDF.

FIGURE 3.1.8. Now each piece of inlay material is cut out with a jeweler's saw and filed as necessary to match the pattern that has been cut out and glued to each Macassar ebony piece. You can see the piece of ebony in the lower right corner of the photo. Each Macassar ebony piece will be individually inlaid.

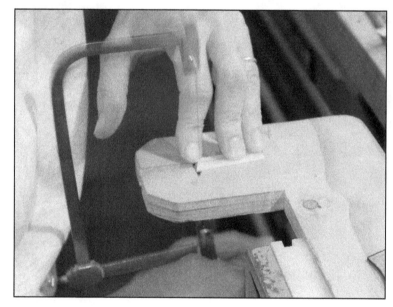

FIGURE 3.1.9. After the pieces are cut, the patterns are cut into the Macassar ebony with a Dremel tool.

FIGURE 3.1.10. Here is one rosette piece with the inlay done. Since the inlay extends slightly beyond the Macassar ebony, it will have to be resanded with the same jigs originally used to create the inside and outside radii.

Each remaining rosette piece will be completed in the same manner.

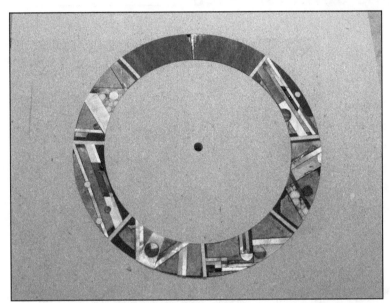

FIGURE 3.1.11. After the inlay is complete and the inside and outside radii have been resanded, the pieces are put together to recheck fit one last time before gluing into the guitar top.

FIGURE 3.1.12. Once we're satisfied with the rosette fit, we cut a 5/8″ grove into the top (at the proper radius, of course), and glue the rosette in. After it dries, we take a 1/16″ router bit and cut a groove around the inside and outside radii of the rosette (cutting partially into the rosette and partially into the top).

FIGURE 3.1.13. After the 1/16" slots are cut, purflings of black fiber, maple, and black fiber are glued into the slots. Here is the final rosette—all glued up and put through the sander.

THE CLASSICAL GUITAR BRACES

FIGURE 3.1.14. Now that the rosette is complete and the top is sanded to its proper thickness (approximately .090), we cut out the sound hole (like we did on the steel string), turn the top over so the underside is up, and mark the position of the braces. In the photo, the braces have been brought to their basic widths and heights (see drawing 3.1.2 for the actual dimensions of our braces) and are ready to glue.

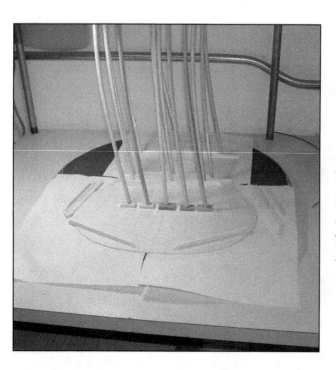

FIGURE 3.1.15. We start gluing the upper and lower face braces (above and below the sound hole), the diagonal strut, and the bridge plate. We will need the bridge plate glued to mark and notch the braces that will go over the bridge plate.

FIGURE 3.1.16. As you can see, we have given a shape to the ends of the braces using a belt sander. It's easier to do on the belt sander before gluing than with a chisel or plane after it's glued down. We then hold the brace on its respective line and mark where it crosses the bridge plate. Both sides must be marked.

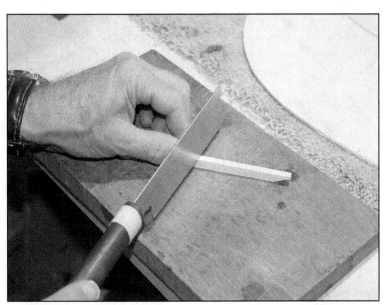

FIGURE 3.1.17. We now connect the marks on each side of the brace and saw a shallow cut into the brace on each of the lines.

FIGURE 3.1.18. Now we use the chisel to cut out the notch. If it's not deep enough, we will extend the cut lines on each side slightly and make it deeper. Try not to make the notch too deep—we want the brace to fit exactly on the guitar top and the notch exactly on the bridge plate.

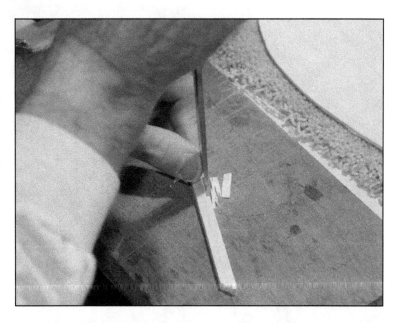

FIGURE 3.1.19. Here is a close-up of one of the braces as it crosses the bridge plate.

FIGURE 3.1.20. All the fan braces are glued down and all the pencil lines have been erased.

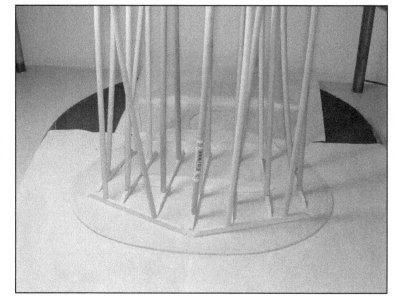

FIGURE 3.1.21. We will carve the braces using a curved-sole plane held at an angle. The brace on the right has been carved to a peak at the top. This keeps the bulk of the brace's strength while taking away much of its weight.

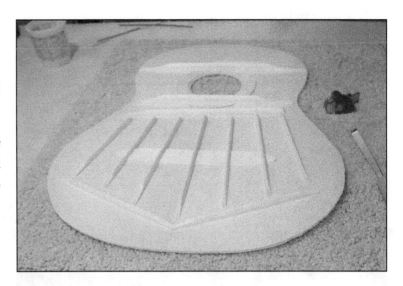

FIGURE 3.1.22. Here is the top, completed with the braces all carved, ready to sign.

The classical back is done in the same manner as our steel string back, so we will not go into any additional detail on its construction.

THE CLASSICAL SIDES

We are starting with two book-matched sides of Brazilian rosewood for this guitar, and we prepare them for the Fox bender. The only difference between this job and the steel string is that this classical was ordered with a cutaway, so we have a Fox bender with a cutaway attachment.

FIGURE 3.1.23. Here is the bender, ready to go. The side is at the lower right, and it has been sprayed with water and folded in a piece of parchment paper. Next, the aluminum foil, seen at the lower left, will be folded around the parchment paper to keep the moisture in during bending. The two springs in the bender help push against the cutaway plunger and keep the wood from cracking.

FIGURE 3.1.24. Diana is pressing in the cutaway. This is done very slowly, after the heat blanket has been brought to full temperature. The waist is done first, then the cutaway, and lastly, the lower bout.

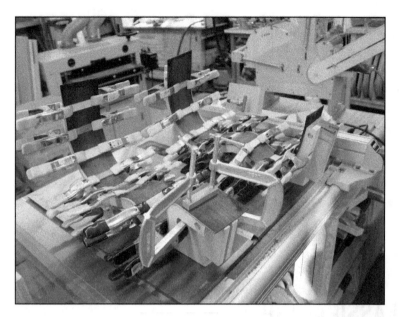

FIGURE 3.1.25. Here are both sides of the classical guitar. The cutaway is in the foreground, and the noncutaway is in the background. Note that if the sides do not fit comfortably into the molds, they may have to be heated over a hot pipe to make them fit. They should not be forced into the molds if they don't fit. For an excellent description of pipe bending, see Guitarmaking Tradition and Technology, by William R. Cumpiano and Jonathan D. Natelson

FIGURE 3.1.26. After the ends have been trimmed, they will fit tightly together before gluing the headblock and tailblock. Similar to the steel string, we use a similar jig to sand the proper radius onto the headblock. In addition, the cutaway is designed to come off the headblock at a 90-degree angle, so the headblock is fairly simple to make.

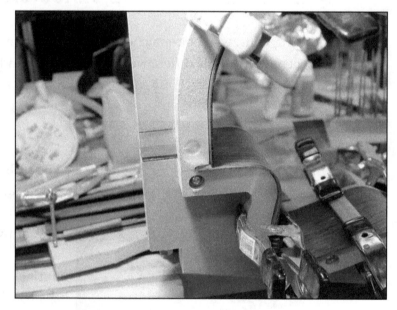

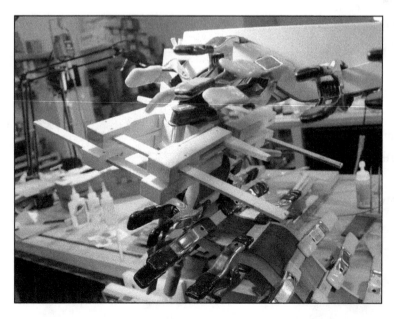

FIGURE 3.1.27. This figure is very busy, so here is what we're showing. The headblock is glued to the sides, and the four cam clamps are clamping the block to the noncutaway side, at the head of the guitar. The steel Bessey clamp is holding the block down against the cutaway portion of the side.

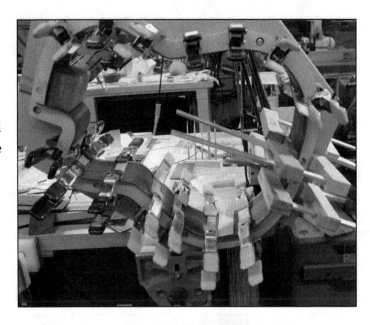

FIGURE 3.1.28. The headblock is glued in, and the tailblock is being clamped as it was for the steel string guitar.

FIGURE 3.1.29. Next, the kerf and Popsicle sticks are glued on in the same manner as the steel string and archtop guitars. We will not go into any additional detail here.

FIGURE 3.1.30. After the kerf, the rest of the steps to put the body together are the same as those of the steel string, except there are fewer braces to tie into the kerf than there are on the steel string. The back is being glued to the sides in the figure. The top is glued on next, followed by the end graft and bindings.

FIGURE 3.1.31. Here is the classical body, binding being scraped.

FIGS. 3.1.32 AND 3.1.33 Show the completed classical body, ready for final sanding and finishing.

FIGURE 3.1.32.

FIGURE 3.1.33.

3.2
THE CLASSICAL NECK

As is the case with the archtop neck, the classical neck has the same initial steps as the steel string neck with three exceptions: scale length (this classical scale length is 650 mm), width of the classical fingerboard (typically about 2" but in our case 1 15/16"), and we don't typically put the carbon fiber rods in our classical necks. With the reduced tension of the nylon strings, there is no reason to. However, we always put a truss rod in every guitar. In our opinion, it just makes sense. We've seen too many good classical guitars come into our shop for repairs because the neck has started to bow over time, even with the reduced string tension. We don't want that to happen.

This classical guitar will have a raised fingerboard at the customer's request. In this case, the neck angle is significantly different from that of the steel string and the archtop. In the case of the steel string, the neck angle is tilted back about 1.5 to 2 degrees. In the case of the archtop, it is tilted back about 4 degrees. However, in the case of a raised fingerboard classical, the neck is tilted forward about 2 degrees. Before attempting this kind of design, you must draw the side cross-section of the guitar, including the arch of the top (in our case, it's the same as the steel string, 25'). Getting the neck angle right is very critical. Since there is a raised fingerboard, the construction of the neck is very similar to that of the archtop with the fingerboard extension.

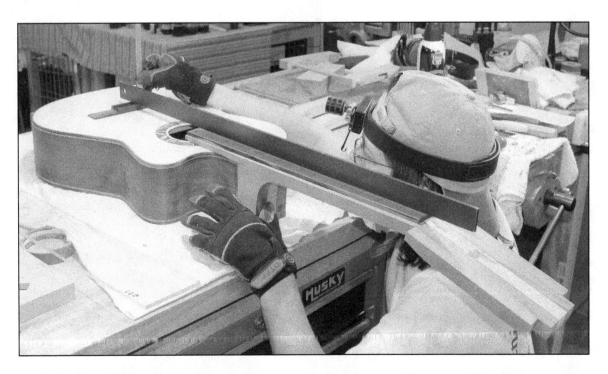

FIGURE 3.2.1. After the neck is shaped, the router table is used to cut out the ledge for the fingerboard extension. In our case, it will be 3/8″ tall. The other dimensions are set by the width of the neck and the length of the fingerboard.

FIGURE 3.2.2. This shows the same method we used on the archtop to measure the fit between the guitar top and the fingerboard extension. Once the pencil line is made, the extension is trimmed down to the line with a chisel, a plane, or both. (Also check Figure 2.2.12 on the archtop neck fit to check the technique.)

FIGURE 3.2.3. This is a small, curved-sole plane being used to shape the underside of the fingerboard extension. Once we have a basic shape, we will carve out the center portion so the only part we have to fit to the top are the outer edges (about 1/8″ wide each).

FIGURE 3.2.4. After initially shaping the fingerboard extension, we start to drop the dovetail into its slot. As we carve the dovetail, we continuously check the neck alignment from left to right (as we did on the steel string and the archtop) and vertically by putting the fingerboard down on the neck (it's not glued on yet), using a straight-edge to check its height against the bridge. We want the height to align lower than it does with the steel string—about 1/8″ below the top of the bridge in this case (without the saddle). The classical alignment is lower on

the bridge, because typically, classical players like their action significantly higher than that of a steel string player. This will keep the saddle from being too high.

FIGURE 3.2.5. As the neck gets down into the dovetail, sandpaper is used to get the underside of the fingerboard extension to meet exactly with the top.

FIGURE 3.2.6. In addition, to be sure the left to right alignment is correct, we will pull some sandpaper on one side or the other, depending on the misalignment. We want to get this alignment as close as we can before we glue on the fingerboard.

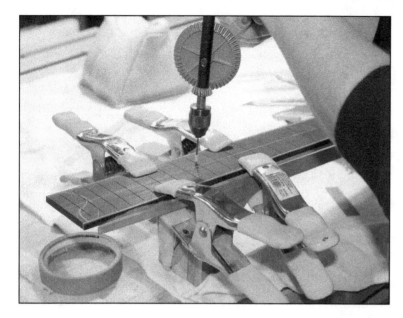

FIGURE 3.2.7. Once we have the alignment close, we're ready to glue down the fingerboard. We drill our pin alignment holes in the first and eleventh frets (as opposed to the first and thirteenth frets) and glue down the fingerboard, just as we did with the steel string.

FIGURE 3.2.8. Here is the fingerboard, glued down, along with the headstock veneer.

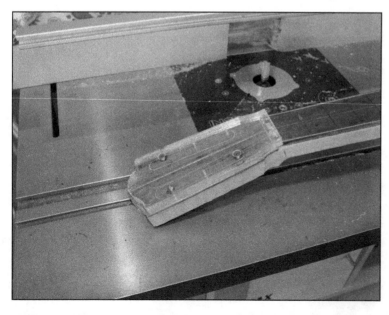

FIGURE 3.2.9. We have the headstock template screwed to the headstock. We've band sawed closely around the template and the fingerboard, and we're ready to rout the final shape. Note that we have put the screws into the headstock in the area where the slots will be routed out.

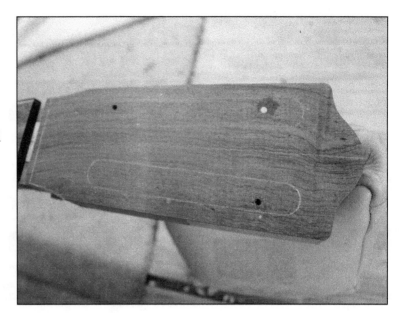

FIGURE 3.2.10. Here is the headstock, all shaped.

FIGURE 3.2.11. As with the steel string, we sand down the back of the headstock to final thickness. Note that the spacer under the headstock is thinner than the one for the steel string (Figure 1.4.106). This gives us a headstock thickness of about 1/32″ over 3/4″ (29/32″)

FIGURE 3.2.12. Now we drill the holes for the tuning machines. The jig shown is a tuning machine drill jig for slotted pegheads from Stew-Mac. Note that we have a depth stop on the bit, so we don't go too deep.

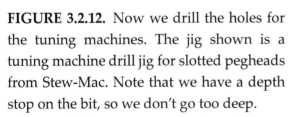

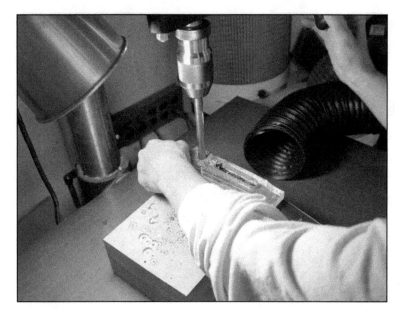

FIGURE 3.2.13. We have put a new template onto the headstock that is the same size as the one we used to cut it originally to shape. This template is put down with double-sided tape. In the figure, multiple holes are being drilled into what will become the headstock slots to make routing the slots easier.

FIGURE 3.2.14. Using a small laminate trimmer with a 3/8″ bit with a flush-trim bearing, we are able to follow the inside edges of the template and cut the slots for the tuning machines.

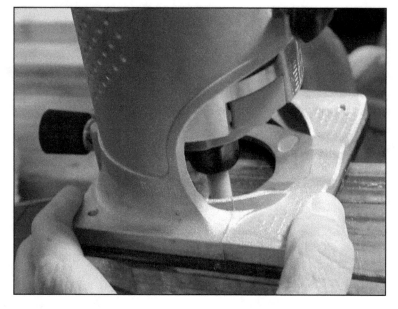

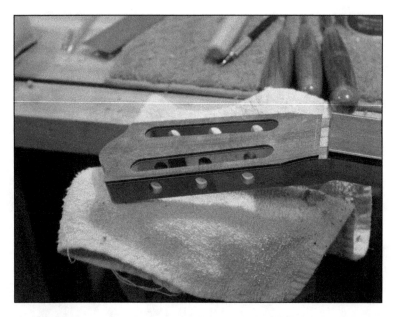

FIGURE 3.2.15. Here is the headstock after the holes and slots have been cut. The dark square on the inside of the slot is the veneer between the mahogany and the maple on the neck.

FIGURE 3.2.16. Now we have to file the slanted edges onto the slots. The slots are 5/8″ wide, and we are using a 1/2″ file. Note the tape on the inside edges of the slots. It is obviously there to protect the slots from file marks. However, you must be careful because it is still easy to scratch the wood through the tape.

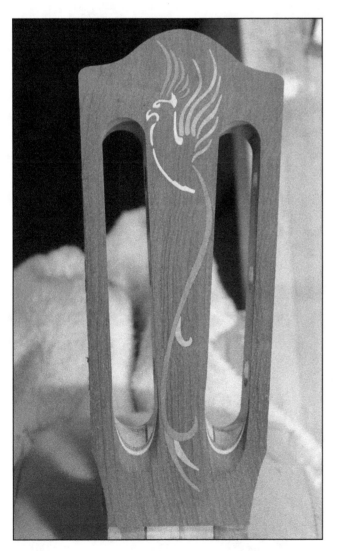

FIGURE 3.2.17. Here is the final headstock, slots all done, along with inlay. The inlay was done in the same manner as the steel string inlay. Many classical guitars don't have an inlay on the headstock, but our customer wanted our logo inlaid in wood so it would be more subtle than our normal inlay of MOP and abalone shell.

Our customer wanted a steel string/jazz style profile on the back of the neck, so its profile is an arc, which was calculated in the same manner as the steel string and archtop neck profiles were. If you want a true classical-style profile, the best way to get that is to use an existing classical neck, and put a contour gauge on it (at several points along the neck), and transfer these profiles to a piece of cardboard or 1/8" MDF. This can then be used as the template you will use as the neck is being carved.

DRAWING 3.3.1 The Classical Guitar Neck Profile.

JAZZ CLASSICAL NECK PROFILE
"C" SHAPE

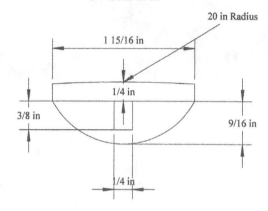

STANDARD CLASSICAL NECK PROFILE
"D" SHAPE

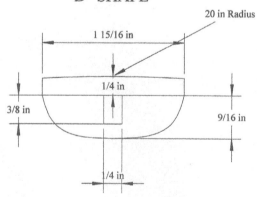

3.3
THE CLASSICAL BRIDGE

We start the classical bridge by making a bridge blank the same way we make the steel string bridge blank. We create a blank 7 1/4″ long, 1 1/8″ wide, and 3/8″ thick. We will typically make about a dozen classical bridges at a time because they're more time-intensive to make than the steel string bridge.

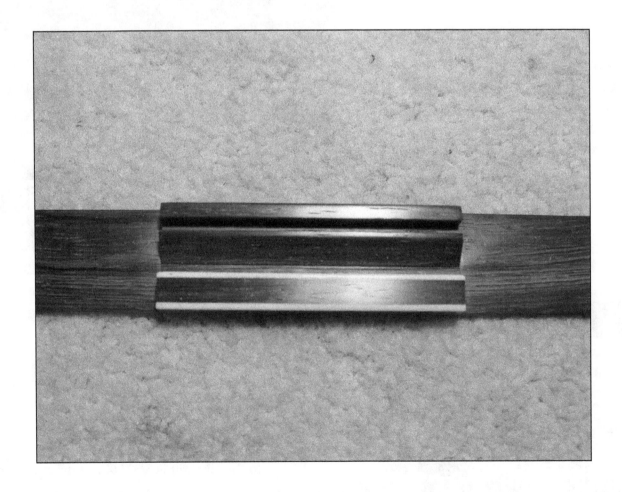

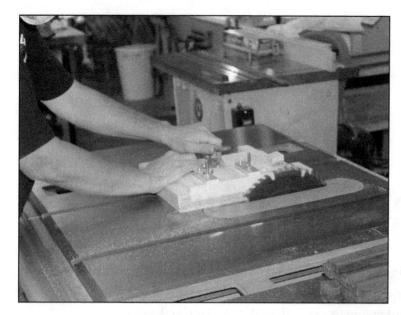

FIGURE 3.3.1. Diana has completed all the rosewood bridge blanks using a jig very similar the jig used for this purpose on the steel string bridge. She is making the last of two bridge blanks of poplar, which will be used as trial pieces to be sure we have all the cuts right. The blank is 7 1/4″ (185 mm) long, 1 1/8″ (29 mm) wide, and 3/8″ (10 mm) tall.

FIGURE 3.3.2. Starting with one of the poplar blanks, the first cut is made. It is being shown as it goes through the table saw. This cut defines the tie block and is 1/4″ deep (5.5 mm), and the edge is 3/8″ (10 mm) from the back of the block. Once we are happy with this cut, all the blocks will be cut the same.

FIGURE 3.3.3. Here is the bridge blank after the first four cuts. The two small cuts to the far left are 3/64″ wide (1.2 mm) and 3/64″ deep and are intended for the tie block decorative strips (more on those later). The cut to the far right is 5/32″ (4mm) from the right edge of the blank, and it is 1/8″ (3.2 mm) wide (the thickness of the saw blade). It is the saddle slot. This cut is 3/16″ (4.75 mm) deep.

FIGURE 3.3.4. This shows the final cut made on the table saw. We slant the blade to a 45-degree angle and cut the block between the saddle slot and the tie block. This cut is made to allow the strings to travel straight from the holes in the tie block to the top of the saddle.

FIGURE 3.3.5. This shows one of the rosewood bridges with the angle cut.

FIGURE 3.3.6. Here is the jig we use to cut the wings of the bridges. The wings are exactly 2″ in length because the longest router bits that we can easily find (and for a reasonable price) are 2″ long.

FIGURE 3.3.7. Here is the wing cut, made on one of the poplar bridge blanks.

FIGURE 3.3.8. Here is the classical bridge for this book. It is made of Brazilian rosewood. It is starting to look pretty good.

FIGURE 3.3.9. Now, Diana finds the center point of the bridge. In addition, knowing that the outer string spacing will be 2 5/16" (based on the neck width), she will mark the points where the outer strings are located.

FIGURE 3.3.10. Using a Stew-Mac string spacing ruler, Diana finds the outer string position and then marks the position of the rest of the strings. We then make a mark 1/8" to the bass side of each string since we are making a two-hole tie system for this guitar. We also mark the centerline horizontally along the back of the tie block. Figure 3.3.11. We are now ready to drill. In this photo, the depth stop for the drill press is being set to allow the bit to bass through the tie block but not touch the angle.

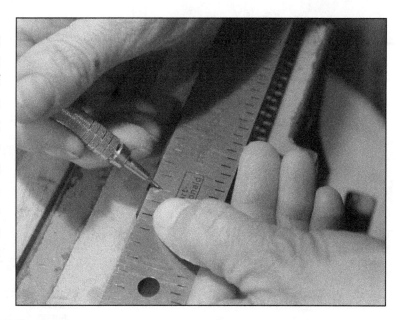

FIGURE 3.3.12. Time to drill.

FIGURE 3.3.13. Now we put the decorative pieces on the tie blocks. They are pieces of bone, available from LMI. They are approximately 1/16" X 1/16" X 3 1/2". They are taped in place and will be superglued down.

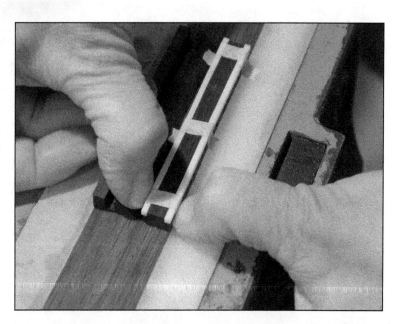

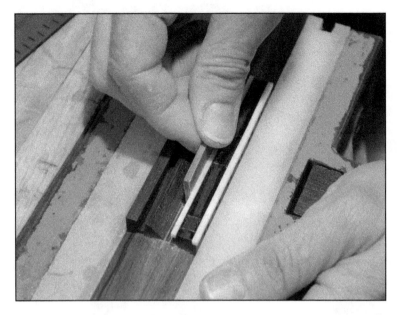

FIGURE 3.3.14. Using a thin, custom-made sanding block, we sand the front edge of the tie block bone piece since it slightly overhangs the wood of the tie block.

FIG, 3.3.15. Now, the top of the block is sanded.

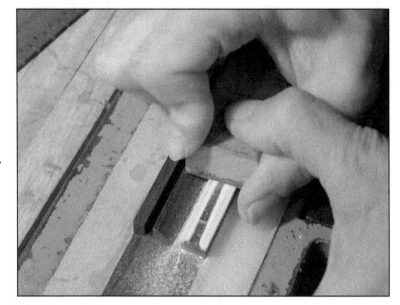

FIGURE 3.3.16. After sanding and filing the ends of the blocks, we sand the edges of the bone pieces to soften them so they will not break strings, since strings will certainly pull very hard across the top of the back block.

FIGURE 3.3.17. Next, we sand the 25′ radius onto the bottom of the bridge using the same radius sanding block we used for the steel string bridge.

FIGURE 3.3.18. After some sanding, the bottom of the bridge is chalked and resanded to check progress. The photo shows there is more sanding to be done. Once the bottom of the bridge is completed, the top of the bridge is sanded from 220 grit to about 600 grit.

FIGURE 3.3.19. Once this level of fine sanding is done, we buff the bridge. We will not be putting a finish on the bridge, but sanding and buffing it will almost make it look finished.

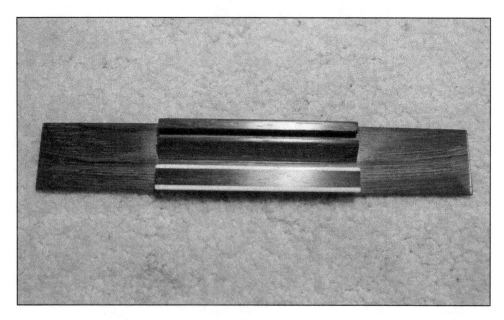

FIG, 3.3.20. Here is the final bridge. Note the taper at the edges of the wings (you can particularly see it on the right side). That taper was done by hand with a file and a sanding block.

3.4
THE CLASSICAL GUITAR: FINAL ASSEMBLY

We've skipped over the finishing of the classical guitar because it is the same as the finish process of the steel string guitar (without the sunburst). We will start our discussion of the final assembly process after finish and buffing are complete, and we have peeled off the tape from under the fingerboard and the bridge.

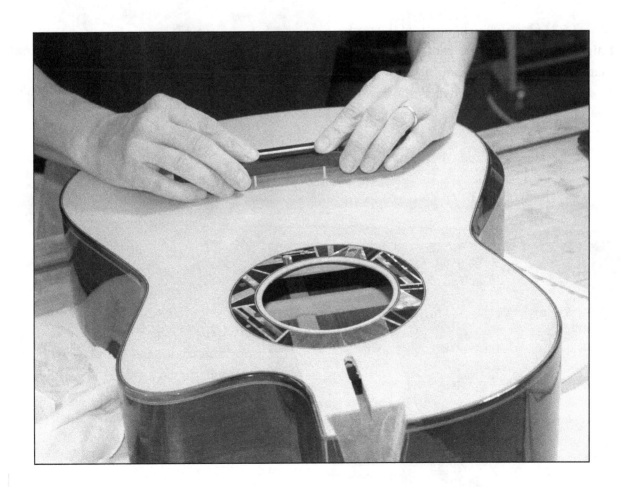

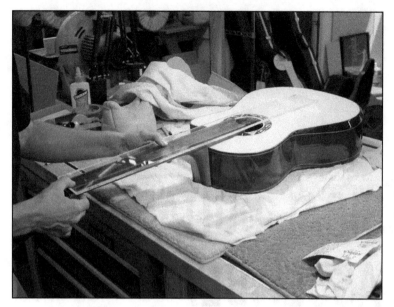

FIGURE 3.4.1. We start by clamping on the neck and checking the alignment. We use a homemade template made of plexiglass 1/4″ thick, 3″ wide, and about 30″ long. It has a centerline scratched on it, and two other lines that approximate the position of the two outside strings. Two holes (5/64″ in diameter) are drilled in the template exactly where the two outer strings intersect the saddle.

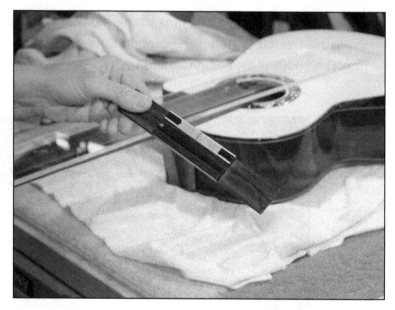

FIGURE 3.4.2. Once we're happy that the neck is straight by checking the centerline of the template with the center seam of the top, we put a piece of tape on the bridge as shown and mark a centerline on it.

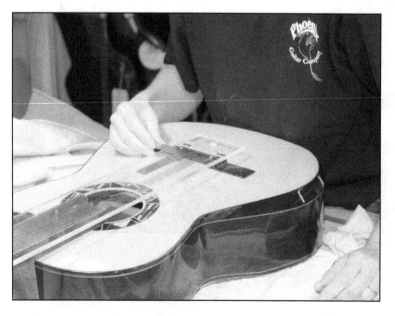

FIGURE 3.4.3. We place the bridge in position under the template with the holes aligned directly over the saddle slot, and check that the bridge is perpendicular to the template centerline with a small square.

FIGURE 3.4.4. When the position of the bridge is right (meaning it's square to the centerline, and the holes line up correctly in the saddle slot), we drill holes directly through the template holes, through the saddle slot and through the guitar top.

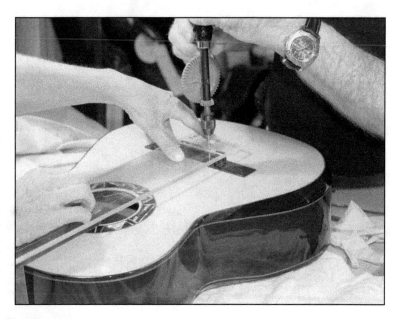

FIGURE 3.4.5. We now insert a portion of a wooden toothpick into each hole. The toothpicks should fit snugly into the holes, with no wiggle room. You must find the right size toothpicks or tiny wooden dowels (you can get 1/16″ dowels, which are really about 3/32″—and you may have to use 3/32″ holes in this case) before you drill. It is imperative that the toothpicks or dowels are tight in the holes.

FIGURE 3.4.6. We will use the toothpicks, just as we used the brass pins on the steel string bridge, to hold the bridge tightly while we scribe around the bridge.

FIGURE 3.4.7. Once we've completed the scribe line, we chisel away the finish to the scribe line.

FIGURE 3.4.8. We now repeat the process of scribing and chiseling the finish under the fingerboard.

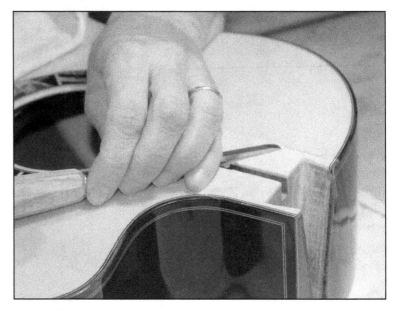

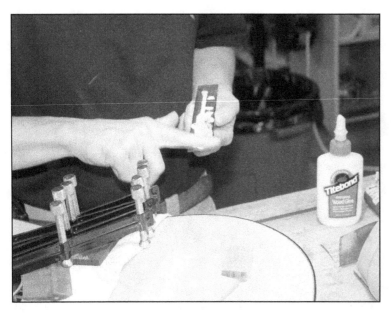

FIGURE 3.4.9. Glue is being put onto the bridge.

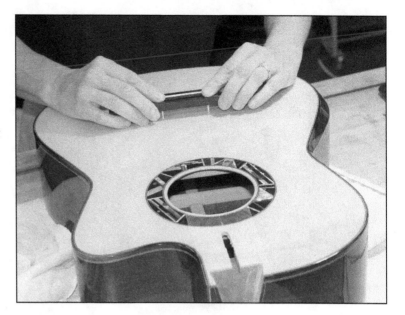

FIGURE 3.4.10. The bridge is being put down directly onto the toothpicks.

FIGURE 3.4.11. Time to put on clamps. First we put down three cauls, one over each wing, and one in the center. Then we like to use four clamps as shown.

FIGURE 3.4.12. A plastic straw is being used to scrape up most of the glue squeeze-out.

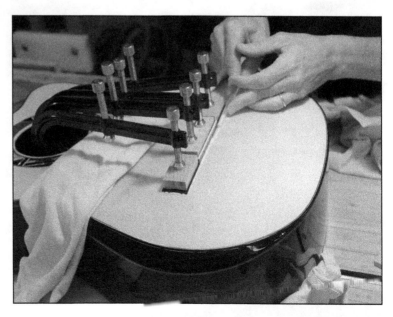

FIGURE 3.4.13. Then a damp cloth is used to wipe up the rest.

FIGURE 3.4.14. While the bridge dries, we start on the fret job. Just like with the archtop, we're going to fret the fingerboard off the guitar. We could wait and do it on the guitar, as we did with the steel string, but this is easier to do. Since this top is significantly thinner than the top of the steel string, we don't want to risk pounding frets on the guitar.

FIGURE 3.4.15. The frets over the fingerboard extension are pounded in using the bag of lead shot to stabilize the shock.

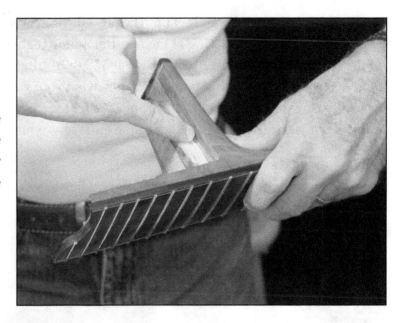

FIGS. 3.4.16 AND 3.4.17. Now it's time to glue on the neck. Glue is spread on the fingerboard extension (note only the outer edges will be in contact with the top) and the dovetail surfaces.

FIGURE 3.4.18. The neck is glued and clamped as shown.

FIGURE 3.4.19. After the neck is dry, the remainder of the fret job is completed. Fret leveling, crowning, and polishing are done the same way as on the steel string. The neck is now buffed. Note that the top of the guitar is protected during these steps.

Finally, the guitar is strung and set up. The procedure is the same as it was for the steel string. However, we tend to make the string spacing at the first fret a little higher. We use .012 at the low E and A strings, .011 for the D and G strings, and .010 for the B and high E strings. Also, the action at the twelfth fret is typically higher on a classical. For this, you must know what your customer wants before you build the guitar. If he wants very low action (8 or 9/64ths), the neck will be set at an angle very different than if he wants 12/64ths. Many of our jazz customers like their action quite low, while classical customers tend to want much higher action.

FIGURE 3.4.20. This is Marty Ashby. We built the classical guitar in this book for Marty. He has won multiple Grammys as a guitarist and producer, and is the Executive Producer of MCG Jazz, a program of the Manchester Craftsmen's Guild in Pittsburgh. He stopped by our shop one afternoon a few years ago when he was preparing for a gig at the Musical Instrument Museum in Phoenix. He heard that we made archtops and needed to borrow one for his upcoming gig. He didn't want to travel with one. We loaned him a guitar that day and on several occasions following that one. It was always great having him stop by the shop. Truly, a master musician, we went to every gig he had in town until I moved to California. Eventually, Marty ordered an archtop (the one on the back cover of this book), and a year or two later, he ordered this classical. It was a real pleasure working on these guitars and getting to know Marty.

IMPORTANT REFERENCE MATERIAL

This short list of books are the ones that I think are some of the best and should be in any guitar maker's library.

1. *Guitarmaking Tradition and Technology*, by William R. Cumpiano and Jonathan D. Natelson—a great general reference, and an excellent description of both steel string guitar, and Spanish style classical guitar construction.

2. *Making an Archtop Guitar*, by Robert Benedetto—another great reference by one of the premier archtop builders of all time.

3. *Making Master Guitars*, by Roy Courtnall—for the serious classical builder. It gives an excellent description of the bracing techniques of several of the greatest classical guitar builders from Torres to modern time.

INLAY REFERENCES

4. *The Art of Inlay*, by Larry Robinson—an excellent descriptive book by one of the top inlay artists in the world. Larry did the inlay on the millionth Martin, and his work really speaks for itself.

5. *A Guitarmaker's Canvas*, by Grit Laskin—another of the great inlay artists in the world. Grit's work will blow you away, and his techniques are well described.

Printed in the USA
CPSIA information can be obtained
at www.ICGtesting.com
LVHW082307111123
763661LV00096B/4371